D0821757

THE KNACK

STAFF

Editors
Martin Preston
Richard Chapman

Editorial Secretary
Sue Ashby

Art Editors
Maggi Howells
Jonathan Alden

Staff Photographer
Ray Duns

Deputy Editor
Martin Derrick

Projects
Alan Cornish
Clive Padget

Projects Editor
Andrew Kemp

Picture Research
Anne Lyons

Senior Sub Editor
Brenda Marshall

Production Executive
Robert Paulley

Sub Editors
Barry Milton
Trevor Morris
Gregor Ferguson
Tom Hibbert
John Ward

Production Controller
Patrick Holloway

Editorial Assistant
Jill Wiley

Designers
Lee Thomas
Shirin Patel
Christina Fraser
Chris Legee

Cover Design
Jim Bamber

Technical Consultant
George Smith

Production Secretary
Linda Mifsud

Technical Artist
Antonio Toma

Reference Edition published 1984

©MCMLXXX MCMLXXXI MCMLXXXII
Marshall Cavendish Limited
58 Old Compton Street
London W1V 5PA

Printed and bound in Italy by L.E.G.O. S.p.a.

ISBN 0 85685 999 0 (Set)
ISBN 0 85685 996 6 (Vol 22)

The Knack
1. Dwellings—Remodeling—Amateurs'
manuals
I. Chapman, Richard
643'.7   TH4816

ISBN 0-85685-999-0

THE KNACK

THE ILLUSTRATED ENCYCLOPEDIA OF HOME IMPROVEMENTS

Volume 22

Marshall Cavendish · London & New York

Contents

A plywood dinghy –1

Get under way with this low-cost dinghy which is suitable for sails, oars or an outboard motor. Although it is a major undertaking, the finished result is well worth the effort. Part 1 details the construction of the hull

Ray Duns

This basic dinghy will provide an ideal budget introduction to the sport of sailing. Equipped with oars or an outboard, you can use it for fishing or as a general purpose runabout. With a total length of under 2.5m and a low weight, it is easy to transport on top of a car.

Although none of the building is especially difficult, there are a few points to bear in mind. Firstly, you must have a reasonably large, unobstructed work area. Boat construction differs from most other woodwork in some important respects. Since a boat is a collection of compound curves, very few parts will meet at simple angles, and in some cases you will have to resort to eye and judgement to achieve an accurate fit.

Most of the construction is in plywood, which is used for the hull skin and cross members. These are stiffened by the addition of longitudinal timber members. Because the materials will be exposed to water, it is essential to use durable timber. Solid wood parts must be hardwood, and marine plywood is preferable for the boarding. As a cheaper alternative, it is possible to use exterior (WBP) plywood, but this will need more maintenance, and will not last so long. Similarly, you must use waterproof adhesive and brass screws. These are inevitably expensive materials, but there are no cheaper alternatives.

Start by constructing the keel. It will be convenient to prepare a full-size drawing and lay this out flat on the floor. The main keel is in three hardwood sections joined by the centreboard case and with a scarf joint. Join the front sections and shape to a curve. Machine the rear section to the correct profile, then join them with the centreboard case. Add the three posts and the reinforcing braces.

Cut out the three plywood cross members and join them to the keel. Plane the underside of the fore section of the keel to suit the varying angle between the panels. Cut out the two bottom panels, attach the hardwood stringers and then curve over the frame, gluing and screwing in place. Plane the stringers off at an angle then add the upper side panels. You can add temporary braces as necessary to maintain the curve.

Plane off any excess, then turn the hull over and add all the braces and reinforcing strips detailed in the drawings. Fit the foredeck and fill the compartment so formed with foam polyurethane. Fill all cracks and screw heads with waterproof filler, then sand and finish with marine paint and yacht varnish.

Part 2 details fitting out the hull.

Project

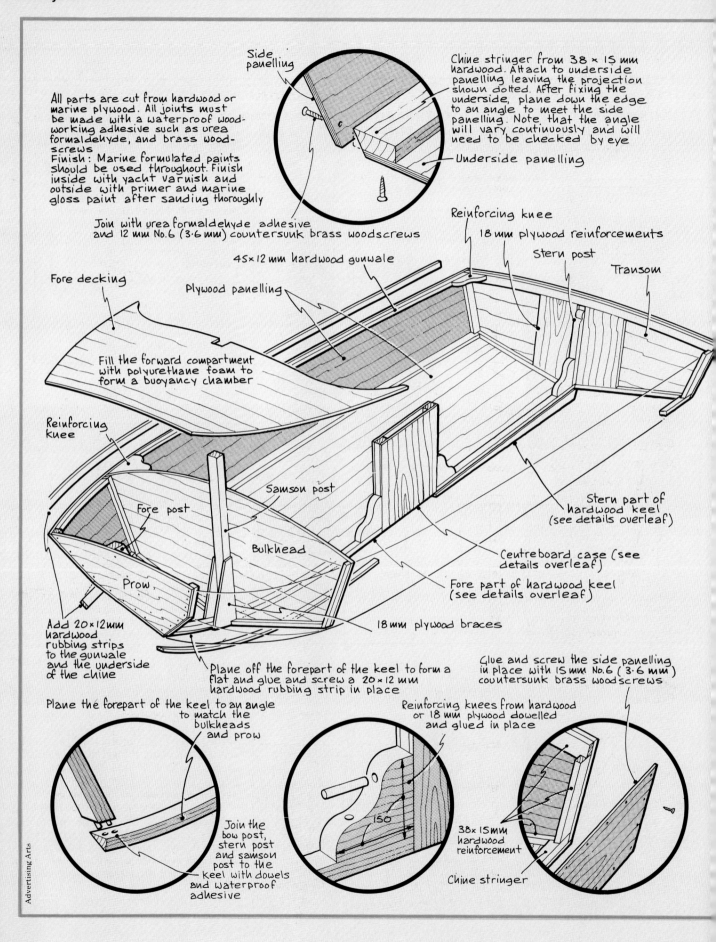

Side panelling

Chine stringer from 38 × 15 mm hardwood. Attach to underside panelling leaving the projection shown dotted. After fixing the underside, plane down the edge to an angle to meet the side panelling. Note that the angle will vary continuously and will need to be checked by eye

All parts are cut from hardwood or marine plywood. All joints must be made with a waterproof wood-working adhesive such as urea formaldehyde, and brass wood-screws
Finish: Marine formulated paints should be used throughout. Finish inside with yacht varnish and outside with primer and marine gloss paint after sanding thoroughly

Underside panelling

Join with urea formaldehyde adhesive and 12 mm No.6 (3·6 mm) countersunk brass woodscrews

Reinforcing knee

18 mm plywood reinforcements

Stern post

Transom

45 × 12 mm hardwood gunwale

Fore decking

Plywood panelling

Fill the forward compartment with polyurethane foam to form a buoyancy chamber

Reinforcing knee

Fore post

Samson post

Bulkhead

Prow

Stern part of hardwood keel (see details overleaf)

Centreboard case (see details overleaf)

Fore part of hardwood keel (see details overleaf)

18 mm plywood braces

Add 20×12mm hardwood rubbing strips to the gunwale and the underside of the chine

Plane off the forepart of the keel to form a flat and glue and screw a 20×12 mm hardwood rubbing strip in place

Glue and screw the side panelling in place with 15 mm No.6 (3·6 mm) countersunk brass woodscrews

Plane the forepart of the keel to an angle to match the bulkheads and prow

Reinforcing knees from hardwood or 18 mm plywood dowelled and glued in place

Join the bow post, stern post and samson post to the keel with dowels and waterproof adhesive

150

38 × 15 mm hardwood reinforcement

Chine stringer

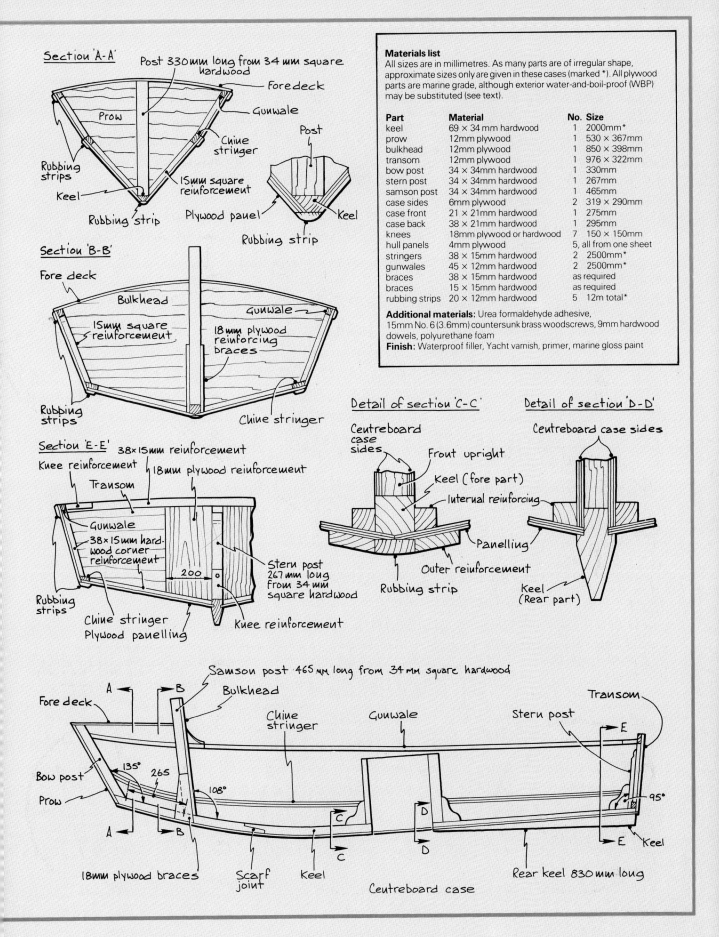

Section 'A-A'

Post 330mm long from 34 mm square hardwood
Foredeck
Prow
Gunwale
Chine stringer
Rubbing strips
Keel
15mm square reinforcement
Rubbing strip
Plywood panel
Post
Keel
Rubbing strip

Materials list
All sizes are in millimetres. As many parts are of irregular shape,
approximate sizes only are given in these cases (marked *). All plywood
parts are marine grade, although exterior water-and-boil-proof (WBP)
may be substituted (see text).

Part	Material	No.	Size
keel	69 × 34 mm hardwood	1	2000mm*
prow	12mm plywood	1	530 × 367mm
bulkhead	12mm plywood	1	850 × 398mm
transom	12mm plywood	1	976 × 322mm
bow post	34 × 34mm hardwood	1	330mm
stern post	34 × 34mm hardwood	1	267mm
samson post	34 × 34mm hardwood	1	465mm
case sides	6mm plywood	2	319 × 290mm
case front	21 × 21mm hardwood	1	275mm
case back	38 × 21mm hardwood	1	295mm
knees	18mm plywood or hardwood	7	150 × 150mm
hull panels	4mm plywood	5, all from one sheet	
stringers	38 × 15mm hardwood	2	2500mm*
gunwales	45 × 12mm hardwood	2	2500mm*
braces	38 × 15mm hardwood	as required	
braces	15 × 15mm hardwood	as required	
rubbing strips	20 × 12mm hardwood	5	12m total*

Additional materials: Urea formaldehyde adhesive,
15mm No. 6 (3.6mm) countersunk brass woodscrews, 9mm hardwood
dowels, polyurethane foam
Finish: Waterproof filler, Yacht varnish, primer, marine gloss paint

Section 'B-B'

Fore deck
Bulkhead
15mm square reinforcement
Gunwale
18mm plywood reinforcing braces
Rubbing strips
Chine stringer

Section 'E-E'
38×15mm reinforcement
Knee reinforcement
18mm plywood reinforcement
Transom
Gunwale
38×15mm hardwood corner reinforcement
200
Stern post 267 mm long from 34 mm square hardwood
Rubbing strips
Chine stringer
Plywood panelling
Knee reinforcement

Detail of section 'C-C'
Centreboard case sides
Front upright
Keel (fore part)
Internal reinforcing
Panelling
Outer reinforcement
Rubbing strip

Detail of section 'D-D'
Centreboard case sides
Keel (Rear part)

Samson post 465 mm long from 34 mm square hardwood
Bulkhead
Fore deck
Chine stringer
Gunwale
Transom
Stern post
A   B
Bow post
Prow
135°
265
108°
A   B
C
C
D
D
E
95°
E
Keel
18mm plywood braces
Scarf joint
Keel
Centreboard case
Rear keel 830mm long

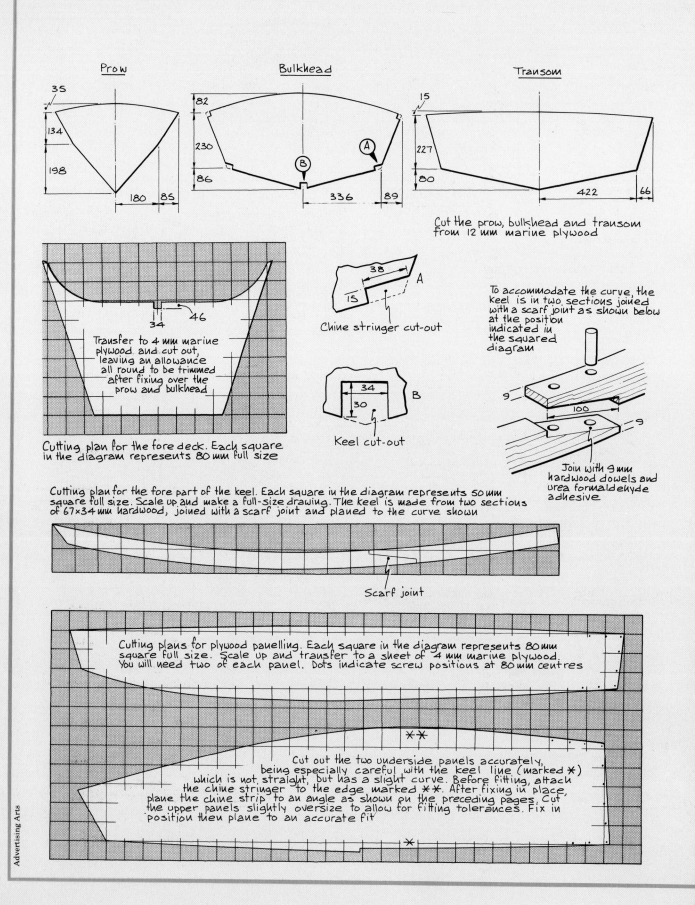

Prow

Bulkhead

Transom

Cut the prow, bulkhead and transom from 12 mm marine plywood

Transfer to 4 mm marine plywood and cut out, leaving an allowance all round to be trimmed after fixing over the prow and bulkhead

Cutting plan for the fore deck. Each square in the diagram represents 80 mm full size

Chine stringer cut-out

Keel cut-out

To accommodate the curve, the keel is in two sections joined with a scarf joint as shown below at the position indicated in the squared diagram

Join with 9mm hardwood dowels and urea formaldehyde adhesive

Cutting plan for the fore part of the keel. Each square in the diagram represents 50 mm square full size. Scale up and make a full-size drawing. The keel is made from two sections of 67×34 mm hardwood, joined with a scarf joint and planed to the curve shown

Scarf joint

Cutting plans for plywood panelling. Each square in the diagram represents 80 mm square full size. Scale up and transfer to a sheet of 4 mm marine plywood. You will need two of each panel. Dots indicate screw positions at 80 mm centres

Cut out the two underside panels accurately, being especially careful with the keel line (marked *) which is not straight, but has a slight curve. Before fitting, attach the chine stringer to the edge marked **. After fixing in place, plane the chine strip to an angle as shown on the preceding pages. Cut the upper panels slightly oversize to allow for fitting tolerances. Fix in position then plane to an accurate fit

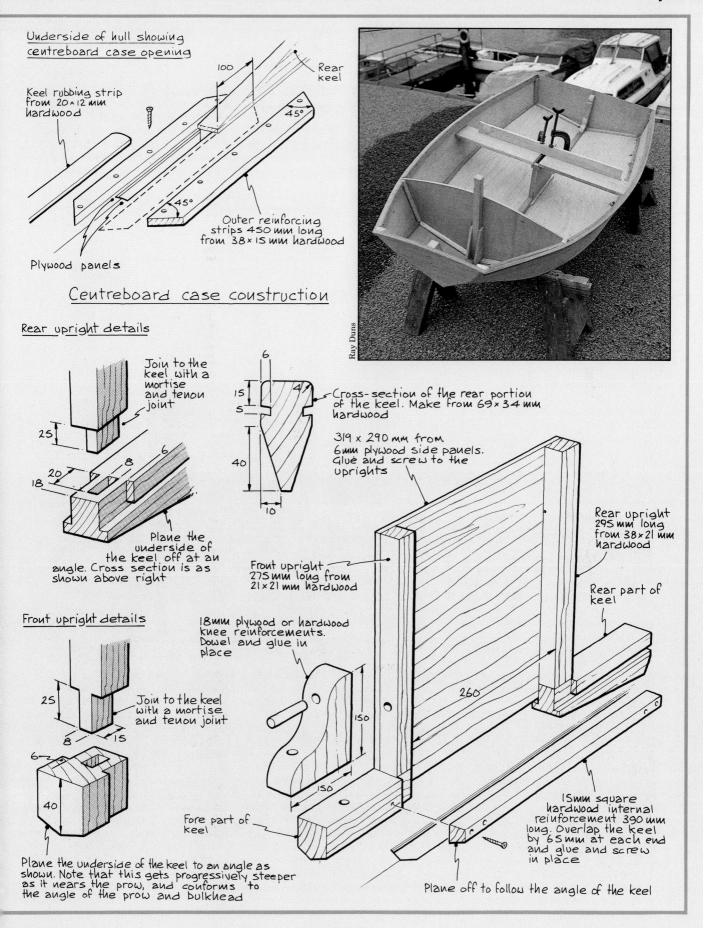

Underside of hull showing centreboard case opening

100

Rear keel

Keel rubbing strip from 20×12 mm hardwood

45°

45°

Outer reinforcing strips 450 mm long from 38×15 mm hardwood

Plywood panels

Ray Duns

Centreboard case construction

Rear upright details

Join to the keel with a mortise and tenon joint

25

8   6

20

18

Plane the underside of the keel off at an angle. Cross section is as shown above right

6

15

5

4

40

10

Cross-section of the rear portion of the keel. Make from 69×34 mm hardwood

319 × 290 mm from 6mm plywood side panels. Glue and screw to the uprights

Rear upright 295 mm long from 38×21 mm hardwood

Front upright 275 mm long from 21×21 mm hardwood

Rear part of keel

Front upright details

25

8   15

6

40

Join to the keel with a mortise and tenon joint

18mm plywood or hardwood knee reinforcements. Dowel and glue in place

150

150

260

Fore part of keel

15mm square hardwood internal reinforcement 390 mm long. Overlap the keel by 65mm at each end and glue and screw in place

Plane off to follow the angle of the keel

Plane the underside of the keel to an angle as shown. Note that this gets progressively steeper as it nears the prow, and conforms to the angle of the prow and bulkhead

Kitchen redesign-2

● **The importance of planning** ● **Laying out the central appliances** ● **Access to fringe appliances** ● **Fitting a twin-tub sink** ● **Installing the services** ● **Data panels for materials and equipment** ● **Cross-referenced index to skills courses**

A Below: *A compact and efficient town kitchen with all the major appliances and services easily accessible*
B. Right: *A country or 'Californian' kitchen with only essential cooking equipment installed: the laundry and deep-freeze are located elsewhere*

Redesigning your kitchen involves a network of decisions about appliances, fittings, services and decorations. This second part of the Home improvements series explains the choices you need to make before settling on your new layout. Bear in mind both what you already have, what you can afford to instal now and also what you may want to include if your family or finances increase.

As explained in part 1 of the series, the most functional kitchens group the essential appliances – sink, cooker and fridge – close together with well-lit, generous work surfaces all around. But kitchens come in as many shapes and sizes as people and each family makes different demands on the room – especially in housing additional equipment. Because of this it is only possible to give guidelines for your improvement scheme, not a formula for the perfect layout. But even so it is worth looking at two successful designs (figs A and B) to see how appliances dictate the space arrangement and what can be achieved with careful planning.

Although part 3 of the series explains how to draw up a plan of action for your improvements scheme, it is useful to keep in mind when considering planning possibilities that 600mm × 600mm is the conventional measurement for depth and width of appliances and furnishings, surfaces and units. Note how this works in the country and town kitchens which, probably like your own room, are not exact multiples of this measurement. Work surfaces cover extra space which can then be used for racks for vegetables, tea towels, or trays. If space is very limited and you are buying new appliances and units, you can find them only 500mm wide or even 500mm deep also, so you can proportionately scale down your kitchen altogether.

Central appliances

However large the range of appliances you intend to include in your kitchen, the priority should be to put sink, cooker and fridge in the most convenient places for each other. Take a fresh look at your existing layout to see which, if any, you need to or are able to move.

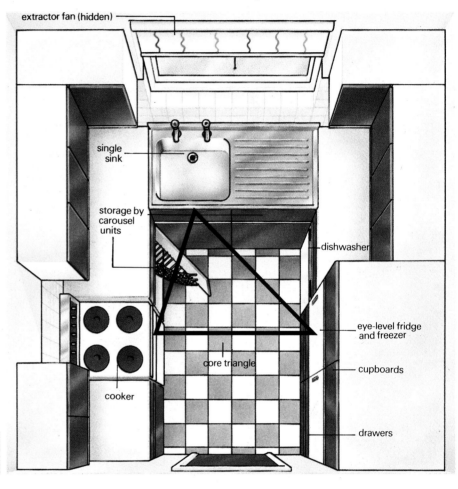

extractor fan (hidden)
single sink
storage by carousel units
dishwasher
eye-level fridge and freezer
core triangle
cupboards
cooker
drawers

Steve Cross

Sinks: If you intend to replace a worn-out sink, think about repositioning it at the same time. Many places other than the conventional outside wall location are feasible by extending the drainage. Radical changes can be made if you can use the 'clearing eye' system, as explained below. However, this will not be necessary if the modification to drainage is minimal. For instance you may be able to move the sink unit much closer to work surfaces, while still retaining a view outside and good lighting, by putting the sink at right angles to its present window wall location. A short move sideways is sometimes necessary to replace a single sink with double bowls. A double sink – even if one is only half-size – is especially

useful if you are installing a waste disposal unit. Always remember that a space for a wall-mounted drainer above the draining board is a great advantage.

Figs 1 to 9 show how to set two bowls into a worktop – including cutting and tiling the worktop, connecting two wastes into a single drain and fitting a mixer tap. Fitting separate bowls or a drainer into a worktop is not only more stylish and adaptable but also considerably cheaper than buying a complete sink unit.

Cooker and fridge: It is rather simpler to move the cooker than the sink, either by repositioning the 30/45 amp socket or by having the gas outlet extended by means of a flexible tube running behind floor cupboards. The same applies to gas and electric fridges.

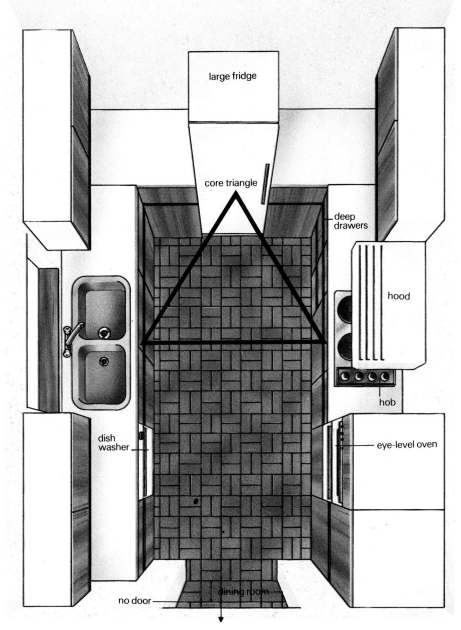

large fridge

core triangle

deep drawers

hood

hob

eye-level oven

dish washer

no door

dining room

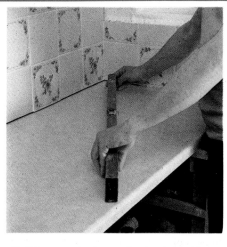

1 *When replacing a single sink with a twin-tub unit start by laying the new worktop in place and checking that it is properly levelled*

2 *Lay the two tubs and the mixer tap you are using in their respective positions and check that the tap reaches both tubs comfortably*

Simon Butcher

3 *Now mark the positions of the tubs on the worktop by drawing a pencil line around the inside of the units as they lie upside down on the surface*

Sometimes you can achieve the best kitchen layout only by placing the fridge and cooker side by side. In this case allow in plans for a 50mm thick board of fire retardant expanded polystyrene to be wedged firmly between the two – but not fixed, as it should be removable for cleaning. The same principle applies to the space-saving arrangement of a bank of built-in appliances with a wall oven above a small fridge. If separate hob and oven are adjacent, there should be a minimum of 300mm setting down space between them. Wall ovens are an especially good choice for anyone who cannot squat easily or if you want to make the kitchen safer for your children. They also allow you more freedom when choosing storage and cooking facilities.

Fringe appliances
Certain other appliances need to be close to the core of the kitchen without interfering with the central work area. These may be items you do not yet have but if you are changing the electrics and furniture in the room, this is the best time to prepare the way for them so you do not have to rip out your current improvements in the near future.

Dishwasher: A dishwasher should be where you can load it while standing at the sink, as dirty crockery needs a preliminary rinse. Also, of course, it has to be plumbed into water supplies and drains. If you have a choice of either side of the sink, choose the side where unloading clean dishes to storage is a simple movement.

Simon Butcher

4 *To cut the apertures, drill a series of 10mm holes inside the pencil line and join them all up using a padsaw. Do not cut outside the circle*

5 *Now lay the tubs in position and check that they fit properly. If their holes are too small enlarge them slightly with a half-round file*

George Wright

6 *If you are fitting a waste disposal unit do it now. Secure the upper part of it to the sink before fitting the rest as described on pages 2290 to 2295*

7 *Now connect the hot and cold water supplies to the mixer tap, and the plastic overflow pipes to the overflow outlets at the backs of the tubs*

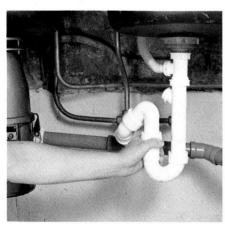

8 *When the waste disposal unit is finally fitted you can connect the waste pipes and traps. Connect both wastes together for convenience*

9 *When all the water supplies and wastes have been connected seal the tubs, the tap unit and the worktop itself with a suitable mastic sealant*

Freezer: If you decide to keep your freezer in the kitchen, do not be bound by the convention of placing it next to the fridge. If you already have a tall fridge and freezer and can only put them side by side, keep the fridge nearest the central core area. The most remote corner of the kitchen is perfectly suitable for a freezer, particularly the top-loading locker type which cannot be used as a worktop.

Washing machine and dryer: These have to be close to each other but as far from the food area as possible. The problem usually lies in drainage, which means any machine not plumbed in to its own separate water supply and waste has to stand next to the sink unless it can be completely disconnected and wheeled away on castors for storage.

A top-loading machine is only suitable for very spacious kitchens though a hinged worktop can be fitted over it. Any machine which discharges its waste via a pipe looped into the sink is unhygienic because germs can come into contact with food so you should try to avoid this.

The most space-saving and hygienic arrangement is a front loading machine plumbed permanently into a fixed waste pipe with a dryer mounted directly over it. But whatever the arrangement of your appliances, if you have to do laundry in the kitchen try to ensure that one worktop area can be reserved exclusively for the clean and dirty washing.

Work surfaces

Give priority to work surfaces over storage – cupboards and shelves can be slotted in to any unused spaces later. Make sure, too, that they are close to the centre of work activities and key appliances. There should be adequate space for food preparation – such as vegetables – near the sink, a place for mixing food, and also a serving area to set down dishes and plates close to the cooker so these do not have to be carried. These can all be combined, as in the town kitchen (fig. A).

However, resist the temptation to have more work surfaces than you really need. The country kitchen (fig. B) has as much as most families will ever need at one time; vast areas created by ranges of floor cupboards just get filled up with items which could better be stored out of sight. The space is better used by installing wall to floor storage, leaving space for a generous kitchen table.

The ideal worktop height depends on the height of the person using it and what they are accustomed to. The average recommended is 900mm and, if in doubt, try this out and vary it between 850mm and 1000mm.

The sink top is best at a slightly higher

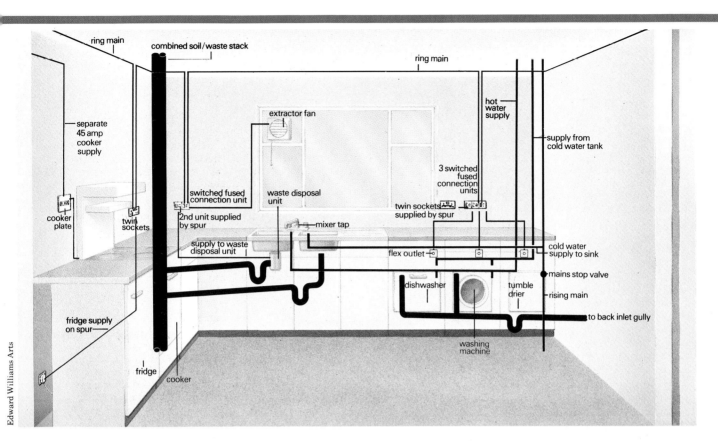

Labels on diagram:
ring main
combined soil/waste stack
ring main
separate 45 amp cooker supply
extractor fan
hot water supply
supply from cold water tank
switched fused connection unit
waste disposal unit
3 switched fused connection units
cooker plate
twin sockets
2nd unit supplied by spur
mixer tap
twin sockets supplied by spur
supply to waste disposal unit
flex outlet
cold water supply to sink
mains stop valve
dishwasher
tumble drier
rising main
fridge supply on spur
to back inlet gully
fridge
cooker
washing machine

Edward Williams Arts

level – 900mm to 1050mm – as arms go over the edge and into the sink. Ideally the bottom of the sink should be comfortably at fingertip level of whoever uses it – but of course, in most families this is impossible.

Solid units are best equipped with simple timber plinths to provide toe space. Plinths are also useful for 'averaging out' units of different heights or for raising 900mm units to a level which suits you better.

Not all kitchen jobs are best done at the standard levels. Standing jobs requiring a down-from-above direction – such as cake or breadmaking – are easiest at a kitchen table or surface of similar height (around 635mm). This can also be a good level for setting a hob into a worktop, as it is easier for stirring, frying or looking into pans. Try to leave knee space under any low work surface as this can be as useful as a table for sitting down food preparation jobs.

Flap down worktops are space-savers in very small kitchens for extra laying out or eating space. But in large kitchens they tend to be left down and accumulate unnecessary objects, so they should be reserved for occasional tasks like ironing. This is also a risk with slide-out cutting boards, and the alternative – often cheaper – is to store these in vertical racks.

One effective way of making the most of a heavily used worktop is to put in a narrow shelf about 250mm above the surface. This is kept free for ingredients and utensils in use during food preparation so these do not clutter up the larger work surface but are spread out ready for use. The shelf should be high enough to clear any mixers or similar equipment used on the work surface but well below wall units which usually start at 1350mm above the ground.

The normal overall depth of most appliances – cookers, fridges and dishwashers is 600mm, and where these form a line with floor units, you need a worktop up to 700mm deep to achieve a smooth run. So decide first on the layout of appliances before buying or making the work surface. Where appliances do not dictate depth and space is limited, a worktop depth of as little as 400mm can be very useful. Remember though that this means storage both above and below has to be much shallower than the conventional units.

Storage
Slot storage into, around, below and above the 'core area' of work surfaces and appliances. Choose either open shelves, cupboards, drawers or hanging racks – or preferably a mixture of all – according to space available and the items to be stored. Your choice should suit the type of cooking you usually do.

C. A typical layout of the services in an L-shaped kitchen showing how the requirements of cooking, washing up and laundry can be accommodated

Wall and floor cupboards already in your kitchen can all be repositioned according to your new layout if you need them. Remember that a work surface does not have to have anything under it and most people find it less strenuous to reach things above 900mm than to bend down. Floor cupboards are most useful for storing large, deep objects which will not fit into a 300mm deep wall cupboard or for anything not frequently used. If you want to use this level for food storage, the only really convenient arrangement is a two storey carousel which makes use of an otherwise difficult corner.

Another sensible use for under work-top space is for deep easy-sliding drawers for storing large but light objects like saucepans and flour sieves. These can be useful either near the sink or the stove. The conventional stack of shallow drawers should be avoided, especially in a small room: only one drawer – for cutlery

> **Warning:** In Australia and New Zealand, service installation – electricity, gas, plumbing – must be entrusted to the relevant licensed qualified tradesmen.

—is absolutely essential; kitchen knives, ladles or stirring spoons can be kept at hand on racks or in jars. Alternatively, rather than waste space under the worktops by installing cupboards or drawers not vitally needed, keep it free for housing trolleys for taking food to other rooms.

The choice between wall cupboards and open shelves depends on taste, cash and practicality. Wall cupboards protect their contents from light, air, heat, steam, dust and grease and also give a smooth, tidy appearance to the kitchen. However they are considerably more expensive than open shelving and the swing of the door can be inconvenient in a very tiny space – although sliding doors overcome this problem. If ventilation is good, open shelves may be equally as useful. Crockery used almost every day does not have time to gather dirt, and the same goes for food; traditional storage containers or modern packaging will keep the contents clean.

Conventional floor and wall cupboards can hold more items if you fix racks on the inside face of the doors.

Fitting heights

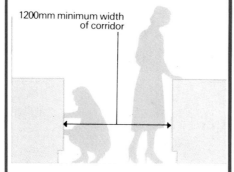

1200mm minimum width of corridor

Fitting heights (from floor)
(recommended for persons of average size)
Work surfaces – including cooker
	850mm to 1000mm
Sink top	900mm to 1050mm
Bottom of wall units above worktop	1350mm
Top of highest unit	1950mm to 2250mm
Highest shelf for general use	1800mm
Minimum floor space between walls of fittings	1200mm

Floor materials

Michael Joseph

Solid concrete floors with a damp-proof course are suitable for all types of flooring—timber, sheeting or tiles—but rigid tiles laid over a timber sub-floor may crack.

Vinyl, linoleum, cork or synthetic rubber

Worktops

Clive Helm/EWA

Materials for kitchen worktops must stand up to hot pans, sharp knives and scouring powders. If you build them yourself they must be easy to cut accurately. As some surfaces are better for certain tasks than others—cutting is best done on a wood surface, pastry making on a cold, flat one—you may prefer to choose a variety of worktops rather than compromising on one all-round work surface.

Base materials (groundwork)
Solid timber: Rare, since it is prone to warping and shrinkage and is relatively expensive to buy.

Chipboard: Cheap and commonly used. Thicker boards are stronger but proportionally heavier. High density boards are the strongest. Amount of support depends largely on type of board and weight to be carried. Needs special fixings, but these are widely available.
Blockboard: Costs more than chipboard. Similar applications, but generally used in better quality work. Any of the common fixing methods are suitable.
Plywood: More expensive than the other materials but good strength in relation to thickness. Waterproof type needed if used in a damp atmosphere or liable to be splashed. All common fixing methods are suitable for plywood.

Surface materials
Ready-made worktops: Available in a wide range of finishes—most commonly laminate and polypropylene—and in standard sizes to fit kitchen units. Very strong owing to the thickness of the material and do not need a great deal of support. However, relatively expensive and difficult to cut, making odd spaces hard to fill. Fixing must be to underside of surfaces.
Ready surfaced boards: Plywood, chipboard or blockboard core with laminate surface. Available in standard sizes, but needs careful cutting to avoid damaging the surface if used to fill smaller gaps. Strength and support required depends on core, chipboard being the weakest. Cut edges must be edged with edging strip or wooden lipping. Fixing must be to underside.
Wood: Hardwoods only are suitable. Attractive, durable if properly maintained, and capable of being refurbished

indefinitely. Strength allows it to form structural part of units below. However, needs frequent sealing (use a vegetable oil on food preparation surfaces) and can work out very expensive. Note that when set on the end grain, wood makes an ideal chopping surface.
Laminate: Hardwearing, waterproof and heat resistant. Available in standard sheets or cut to order in a vast range of colours, patterns and textures. However, quite expensive, fiddly to cut around projections and almost entirely dependent on the groundwork for its strength. Surface prone to scratching and generally impossible to patch, hence the need for a separate chopping board.
Tiles/mosaic: Clean, hardwearing, heat resistant and waterproof if laid properly. Wide range of finishes available and useful for filling odd spaces. However, can be heavy and requires strong and stable groundwork. Non-toxic epoxy grout must be used or joints will harbour dirt. Surface naturally uneven, and separate board required for chopping.
Stainless steel: Sheets can be used to cover groundwork or else arranged over a supporting framework. Durable and easy to clean, but also noisy unless backed with sound absorbent material (such as insulation board) and cannot be used for chopping. Generally too expensive for domestic purposes.

Further reference:
Sheet materials (pages 446 to 452)
Working with chipboard (pages 373 to 379)
Working with laminate (pages 918 to 922)
Ceramic tiling (pages 30 to 36)

in sheet or tile form can be laid directly on to a screed, if smooth enough; otherwise use a 3mm latex screed to level off the base. Fix tongued-and-grooved boarding to battens masonry-nailed into the concrete base. Stick wood block flooring directly on to a level screed. Tiles on a concrete floor need a mortar bed deep enough to give a perfectly level final surface–allow from 2mm for well-cut ceramics to 10mm for quarry tiles.

Boarding spanning a timber sub-floor must be sealed with polyurethane lacquer. Softwood boarding, plywood or chipboard can be left natural or stained or painted first but is also used as a base for sheeting or tiles. Add an extra layer of hardboard when laying vinyl over boarding to stop the joints showing; ceramic tiles need a 25mm blockboard or chipboard base to stop joint movements cracking the tiles.

Timber floors need frequent resealing; tiles may need regrouting at intervals.

Practical properties of flooring
Vinyl: Cheap, hardwearing, easily cleaned, waterproof and resistant to fats and most household chemicals. Available in sheet or tile form in many colours. Texturized vinyl less slippery and shows fewer marks.
Linoleum: Hardwearing but can be damaged by damp and some household chemicals. Expensive and cold. Available in sheet or tile form in strong colours.
Rubber: Hardwearing, resilient and the synthetic type does not smell. Available in sheet or tile form; ribbed or studded types less slippery.
Cork tiles: Exceptionally warm, easy to lay and clean. But prone to chip and needs frequent resealing at worn spots. Also available ready-sealed with vinyl skin, but joints must be sealed after laying.
Carpet: Attracts dirt, so only suitable for kitchen dining areas. Use the looped nylon variety with a foam or latex backing.
Timber: Plywood, chipboard and softwood are cheap but need frequent resealing. Hardwood–strip or parquet–is expensive and needs plenty of maintenance if it is to be kept in prime condition. Not recommended for heavy use.
Tiles: Quarries are hardwearing but also noisy, hard and cold. Attractive natural colouring and impervious to most household liquids. Best laid in a mortar screed, compensating for the irregular depth and shape by varying the joints as you lay. Ordinary ceramic tiles are more uniform but also thinner, and are available in many patterns and shapes. Mosaics often available in panels for easy laying. No seal required on common types of tiles. All tiles are relatively expensive.

Further reference:
Cork tiles (pages 1486 to 1493)
Vinyl flooring (pages 380 to 385)
Quarry tiling (pages 750 to 755)
Mosaic tiling (pages 1774 to 1779)
Levelling concrete floors (pages 666 to 669)
Wood block flooring (pages 936 to 941)
Sanding floors (pages 861 to 863)

Walls and ceilings

Tim Street-Porter

Kitchen decorations must withstand condensation, grease and dirt. Thick, warm coverings – cork or heavy wallpaper – help insulation but where heat loss is serious, add extra insulation material before decorating. Damp cannot be cosmetically disguised so eliminate first. Avoid fire-risk materials.

Most finishes are suitable for both walls and ceilings; walls should be smooth but ceilings can be textured for variety. Very high ceilings with ugly piping can be painted a dark colour and covered by a suspended ceiling or a removable open-structured lower grid; hang lighting on this.

Surfaces
Tiles: Glamorous but expensive and grouting picks up dirt. Good for areas frequently wiped down. Potential problem when sockets outlets do not correspond exactly to tile size.
Timber boarding: Excellent insulation against heat loss and noise. Conceals uneven or crumbling walls. Use gap for wiring and pipes. Treat boards first with damp-proof preservative and fix horizontally, vertically or diagonally on battens pinned to walls at right-angles to board direction. Seal with clear polyurethane lacquer.
Cork: Good insulation and attractive natural colours. Available in wallpaper form (rather fragile), sheet or tiles; ready-sealed tiles easiest to clean.
Washable wallpaper: Vinyl wall coverings are water and steam-proof but shiny. Fungicidal adhesive needed to prevent mould beneath. Washable plastic coated wallpapers have more attractive matt surfaces but are less resistant to water.
Paint: Oil-based and semi-gloss paints–especially with vinyl and polyurethane added–are tougher than ordinary emulsions but can encourage condensation. Anti-condensation paints now becoming available. Prepare wall surface well before painting.

Further reference:
Tiling (pages 30 to 36)
Tongued-and-grooved panelling (pages 278 to 283)
Using cork (pages 1486 to 1493)
Wallpapering (pages 82 to 87)
Painting woodwork (pages 110 to 115)
Colour schemes (pages 386 to 389)
Painting walls and ceilings (pages 430 to 435)

Lighting

Ron Sutherland/EWA

Shadow-free, diffused but bright, illumination is needed in all work areas, including work surfaces, the sink, cooker, and washing machine zone. Additional lighting is useful inside storage cupboards, the cooker and fridge. Dining areas need a softer glow.
Tungsten light bulbs: Cheap and easy to fit. Hang pendent lights from ceiling hooks–as low as possible without hitting heads or cupboard doors–above main work areas. Dimmer switches increase the variety of light intensity.
Spotlights: More expensive and need careful positioning. Tungsten lamps must be totally enclosed to prevent shattering if used in steamy places.
Strip lighting: Tungsten tubes only come in small sizes and emit heat. Fluorescent strips use less electricity, last much longer and are cool. Drawbacks–flickering and a slight hum–are minimized by fixing lights below wall units or shelves, concealed by battens and mounted on rubber washers. Use pull switches near the light source.

Further reference
Kitchen lighting (pages 436 to 441)
Fluorescent lighting (pages 997 to 1003)
Spot and track lighting (pages 2332 to 2337)

Kitchen units and cupboards

Camera Press

Storage units above and below the worktops have a strong bearing on the final look and functioning of the kichen. The great advantage of designing and building your own units rather than opting for proprietary examples is that you can use the walls and floor for support – thereby saving on materials and adding to the design's flexibility.

Closed storage

Cupboards with doors; Generally gives a sleek appearance and enables you to hide kitchen junk. Protects food and other perishables from pests and moisture. Frontages offer a wide range of decorative possibilities. However, generally heavy constructions requiring a fair degree of cabinet-making skills. Doors need opening room and may restrict access to back of units—especially high ones.

Drawers: Similar decorative possibilities to cupboards. Good access to back of units – particularly if on extending runners – and useful for storing small items. However, complicated to construct and fit, and relatively expensive. Most kitchens need fewer drawers than is commonly believed.

Wire basketry: Can be fixed inside cupboards or under worktops to provide better access. Range increasing all the time – pull-out racks, swivelling carousel units for corners – to make better use of space. However, relatively expensive and no good for small items.

Semi-enclosed cupboards: Blinds, curtains and so on provide some measure of screening but are cheaper and more space-saving than doors. However, fabric will collect dirt, so it must be easy to clean.

Sliding doors: Useful where space is limited, but tend to restrict access to unit concerned, are difficult to fit, and harbour dirt in the tracks.

All lower level storage can be incorporated quite easily into a worktop and may even be used to support it. Boxed or frame and panelled constructons may be used, but the latter are the easiest to make – particularly when combined with support battens on the walls and floor.

Open storage

Shelves: Almost infinite variety of styles and sizes possible, combinations work well. Easy to make and relatively cheap, depending on materials. Good access and easy to clean. Can look very effective in more traditional or country-style kitchens. However, can look cluttered unless carefully arranged and generally call for decorative storage accessories. Get dirty easily, and food open to moisture and pests. Generally best suited to higher level storage.

Wirework and racks: As for wirework in cupboards. Relatively expensive, but excellent for storing some items—pots, pans and cups—and can look very attractive.

Many different materials can be used for open storage, but some are better suited to kitchens than others. Solid wood is attractive and durable but also expensive. Using slats rather than solid boards may cut

Ventilation and heating

Gavin Cochrane

Ventilation systems must be capable of handling cooking fumes, smells and steam –and sometimes also dishwasher and washing machine steam. Excess condensation ruins decorations and does long term structural damage, especially to woodwork and plaster.

Fans: Only fans over 225mm diameter can cope with heavy steam. Look for models incorporating speed switches and automatic shutters to block draughts when the fan is off. A window fan is cheaper to instal but noisier and cannot be used when the window is open. Check wall location first for external downpipes or likelihood of nuisance to windows in adjacent rooms.

Extractor hoods: Most efficient type removes bad air and some heat by vent to outside wall, but this is often difficult to instal. Charcoal filter type only recirculates cleansed air and filters need replacing or cleaning regularly.

Kitchen heating is usually only a back-up as cooking generates heat and food requires a cold room temperature. Improve general warmth by double glazing windows and glazed doors not facing the sun. Avoid bulky heaters—such as the electric storage type and old-fashioned radiators.

Central heating radiators: Instal or move wherever layout leaves gaps—but not within 300mm of wall units to prevent warping or damage to cupboard contents. High positions, tall and thin radiators or skirting heating units save space.

Gas: Small outside wall heaters are economical and easy to fit if gas is already in use. Limited location.

Electric: Where necessary small radiant fires or hot air blowers fixed high on walls save space. Guard against trailing flexes by boxing these in or moving socket outlets.

Further reference:
Kitchen ventilation (pages 212 to 217)
Air conditioning (pages 1792 to 1797)

Services

Gavin Cochrane

When you have decided which appliances you are going to instal now and what you want to include in the near future, check your requirements against the existing services. Boxing in extensions to gas or electric wiring may cut down on the overall space available, so take this into account in measuring up and planning.

costs, but needs more support. Blockboard, plywood and melamine veneered chipboard are all cheaper and look good when edged with solid timber. The first two need thorough lacquering for protection. The durability of laminated boards is really wasted on shelving, though these are the easiest to clean.

Supports can be solid or open brackets (possibly on a batten system) but should be permanent – adjustable shelving generally looks too fussy in the kitchen. Metal brackets or wood battens are easy to fit for higher level shelving, but home-made wooden brackets often look better. At a lower level, bricks or blocks make sturdy and cheap supports if the floor is strong enough to take them. The masonry can be sealed or painted afterwards.

Further reference:
Sheet materials (pages 446 to 452)
Box furniture (pages 869 to 875)
Frame furniture (pages 824 to 831)
Interior doors (pages 2320 to 2325)
Working with chipboard (373 to 379)
Shelving systems (pages 1009 to 1013)
Projects:
Modular shelf system (pages 1718 to 1721)
Brick/timber units (pages 2218 to 2221)
Pull-out storage rack (page 693)
Louvre door (pages 1081-1084)
Butcher's block table (pages 2044 to 2047)
Tile-top table (pages 1376 to 1379)
Pine table (pages 598 to 601)

Electrics
Cooker: In the UK, conventional cookers require a 30 amp fixed outlet wired direct to its own fuseway in the consumer unit. A separate hob and wall oven can be powered from two 30 amp outlets or a single 45 amp outlet. Use 6mm² twin and earth PVC sheathed cable for 30 amp installations, 10mm² for 45 amp ones. Most cooker points include an isolating switch and some have an additional 13 amp socket outlet.

Place cooker points above worktop level, near to the appliances, but not obstructing them.

Other appliances: In the UK, these can run off 13 amp sockets or fixed outlets–the latter being safer but less flexible. The golden rule is that sockets must be out of reach of anyone working at the sink.

Plan sockets for smaller appliances just above worktop height, and sockets or fixed outlets for larger appliances below the worktops. If near the sink, position them in cut-outs in backs of units where they cannot easily be touched.

Gas
Installing or modifying any gas supply should be left to professionals after you have chosen sites for the appliances concerned. However, you can speed up installation and cut costs by bearing in mind the plumbing problems – much the same as for water–as you choose the sites.

Plumbing and drainage

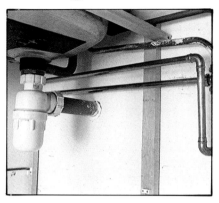

Sink: Reroute existing hot and cold supply pipes as necessary, avoiding sharp bends and inverted U bends which could trap air. Fit stop valves before each tap. Before arranging drainage, consider if other appliances will be plumbed into the sink waste outlet (see below).

Fit a suitable trap to the sink, then run the waste outlet to a gully, single stack, waste stack or sub-stack. In the case of an open gully which is to take waste from other appliances, consider replacing it with a modern back inlet type. Cast-iron stacks are best replaced completely with PVC ones, to which it is easy to fit new branches. Sub-stacks direct to the underground drain are used where more conventional connections are impossible. If you need one, get it installed professionally.

In all cases where the drainage arrangements are altered, consult your local building inspector before starting work. He will be able to give practical advice and will know what drainage arrangements are acceptable in your area.

Washing machine: Cold or hot and cold feeds can be taken from existing supplies, but consult your local authority before teeing off the rising main. Fit stop valves on each feed.

Drainage is normally via a standpipe fitted with a U trap and waste pipe to a back inlet gully or stack. However, some authorities allow the waste outlet to be connected to that of the sink. In this case the outlet pipe must be 50mm diameter; special deep seal traps are available for making the connection. Other authorities allow for more complicated waste outlet runs, providing a clearing eye is fitted for rodding each appliance. Check this point with the building inspector.

Spin drier: Some models with condensers need no plumbing-in. Others require venting via an outside wall or waste outlet (usually the washing machine). Check this point before you buy.

Dishwasher: Much the same requirements as a washing machine (see above).

Waste disposer: Plumbed-in to the sink waste outlet. When plumbing-in to an existing sink, the trap and waste outlet will need alteration.

Note that in a fully equipped kitchen it is not usually possible to run all the appliances through one outlet. However, it is often feasible to run them in pairs – say, sink and dishwasher, washing machine and drier – and connect the two outlets at a single point on the gully or stack.

In all cases, consult the building inspector before committing yourself. Regulations vary widely, and it may be simpler to arrange the drainage than you think.

Further reference:
Drainage (pages 300 to 305 and 406 to 413)
Plumbing-in a washing machine (pages 756 to 760)
Waste disposal units (pages 2290 to 2295)
13 amp outlets (pages 818 to 823)
30 amp outlets (pages 902 to 907)

Refuse disposal

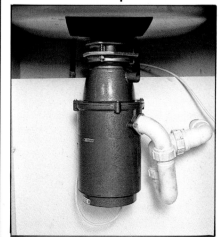

Refuse disposal and storage should be an integral part of the kitchen design. Locate it in the sink area.
Rubbish chutes: Excellent choice, but limited to kitchens where a tile-lined chute can run to bag or bin connected with an outside garbage store.
Waste disposal unit: Takes only 15 per cent of household waste but this includes the worst elements. Noisy and prone to break down if misused. Easy to fit, but needs fast-running cold water and preferably a double sink.
Compost bucket: Good choice for gardeners.
Waste bins and bags: Can be concealed inside sink cupboards. More space required for systems which open automatically.

Further reference:
Fitting a waste disposal unit
(see pages 2290 to 2295)

Glass in the home

Glass has long been valued as the most practical translucent material but now, with a vast range of patterned and coloured varieties available, it can also be used to create unusual and decorative features in the home

Glass is used for a great many functional purposes in and around the home but is often overlooked when it comes to choosing decorative materials. And yet the range of glass available to the home handyman increases every year and can be used in total safety to create interesting and unusual effects that are impossible with more conventional decorating materials.

Types of glass
Much of the glass used in the home is ordinary clear, flat glass which does for everything from glazing windows to providing shelves. Clear glass is the ideal material to use for a wide range of jobs – for admitting light through doors and windows where an uninterrupted view is required, to protect the surfaces of pictures, dressing tables and so on – but where there is a high risk of breakage, either by accident or unauthorized entry, toughened glass is a far safer choice.

Once toughened, glass cannot be cut or drilled and is therefore likely to be too expensive for ordinary glazing jobs where it has to be ordered to size. But for glass doors – especially patio doors and shower screens where standard sized panels can be used – it is a must if only for safety's sake: even if toughened glass fractures under impact, it breaks into small, comparatively harmless pieces rather than the dangerous and unpleasant jagged splinters of plain glass.

Wired glass, which may be clear or textured, is easily cut to size and is also suitable for use in glazed doors, screens

Below: *Differently patterned glass panels in a timber framework create an attractive partition wall with narrow shelves for displaying ornaments*

Right: *An unusual arrangement of glass shelves set across a fixed bathroom window provides room for toiletries and plants without cutting down the light*

Pilkington Flat Glass Ltd

Clive Helm/EWA

and windows where a modest burglar deterrent is needed as well as illumination for the room.

But for the most decorative effects, there is a wide range of patterned, textured and coloured glass available ranging from simple floral designs to bold, chunky geometric patterns. There is something to suit any style of decor, and colours to create different moods and different atmosphere.

Doors and screens

There are plenty of uses for glass around the home, though perhaps doors, screens and partitions, where the glazing admits light to dark corners around the house, are the most obvious. Of course, clear glass admits the maximum light, but the decorative opportunities offered by patterned and coloured glass should not be overlooked.

Glass panels set above or beside door openings are ideal for admitting extra light into a room. Alternatively, small 'windows' set into solid internal walls can borrow light from the brighter room and form an attractive feature too.

Below: *Where the entrance is protected by a porch, tinted glass doors with brass handles are perfectly safe and lend a stylish appearance to the hall*

Jerry Tubby/EWA

For example, you can create a see-through display using a selection of grasses and dried flowers arranged between two closely-spaced panes. Or perhaps have a group of small ornaments on slim glass shelves set into the frame sides and protected by glass in rebates in the outer faces of the frame.

Setting clear or patterned glazed panels into wooden doors is one way of producing a door you can see through. On the other hand, you can have doors made entirely of glass. These come in a range of patterned and tinted designs as well as clear glass and they look particularly attractive hung in pairs between two rooms, providing a useful alternative to sliding doors.

Glass doors come complete with hinges and handles in a range of standard sizes to fit most door openings, and are hung on

Pilkington Flat Glass Ltd

wooden frames just like a traditional door. However, careful measurement is vital when ordering doors of this type, because unlike wooden ones, they cannot be planed off if they bind.

Screens and partitions

Apart from its obvious use in doors, patterned glass is perfect for screens and room dividers to restore some of the privacy lost as larger and larger areas of glazing are installed in many of today's modern homes.

A simple screen using patterned glass offers a degree of privacy while still admitting a certain amount of light. If used with delicate artifical backlighting, it can be made opaque at the flick of a switch. And really clever use of lighting can create stunning or subtle effects according to your mood.

Such screens can easily be made by setting glass into timber frames, installed in bedding putty or sandwiched against foam draught-proofing strip by woven beading to prevent rattling.

Screens and dividers can be used in

Left: *Patterned and coloured glass play an important role in this decorative scheme, adding charm and elegance while still admitting plenty of light*
Below: *A fully glazed wall using glass building blocks gives a decorative yet easily maintained finish—but it is possible only on non-loadbearing walls*

Camera Press

virtually any room in the house to give it extra brightness and colour. For example, a patterned screen in cool green tinted glass could provide a perfect division between a kitchen and dining room. Equally you could create a warm and welcoming atmosphere in the living room using a screen of amber patterned glass with subtle backlighting.

Furniture and decorative effects

Glass can be used in a variety of ways in furniture construction and suits any style of decor. Smoked glass is very fashionable for modern furniture, while plain glass cut into small leaded panes in a framed door looks most attractive in period or reproduction furniture.

Glass shelves, whether plain or coloured, look good when lit from above or the sides by concealed lighting so that the light shines through to illuminate the entire display. Glass is also ideal for sliding or hinged doors to keep the dust out of bookshelves or display cabinets.

On tabletops, toughened glass makes an attractive surface which can withstand fairly high temperatures. Clear, patterned or coloured glass is equally suited for occasional or dining tables set in wood or metal frames.

Glass is an excellent material for protecting vulnerable surfaces that you still want on show. Antique tables, dressing tables, and chests of drawers for instance, can all be fitted with plate glass overlays, cut exactly to suit their dimensions.

Clear glass also provides a perfect splashback over delicate wallpaper and other fragile wall decorations, but should not be screwed too tightly against an uneven wall surface or it may crack.

For protecting pictures and prints, without glare marring your enjoyment of the work, there is a special non-reflecting glass (diffuse reflection glass) which cuts out glare entirely. It is rather more expensive than ordinary float glass and is generally available from picture framers rather than glass merchants.

A novel way of using glass in the home is in the form of hollow glass blocks. These are widely used in public buildings, but are also available – if not in such a wide range of colours and sizes as to architects — to the home handyman.

These blocks look particularly striking used in moderation for screens, porches and dividing walls. However, they are not usually loadbearing, which means there is a limit to the size of wall you can

construct with them. The blocks can be built up using either conventional mortar joints, just like any other building blocks, or a dry-fixing method of flexible 'gasket' strips (usually available with the blocks).

Whether you are using glass in doors, screens or windows, do not feel restricted to the shape of your door, window or partition frames. You can create more unusual outlines containing curves and irregular shapes by facing frames with plywood masks. Break up the appearance of large glass panes by gluing thin wooden or plastic mouldings to both faces of the glass to create the look of a multi-paned window.

Alternatively, use imitation lead strips to give the appearance of leaded lights –

perhaps even going so far as to use glass paints to make the pane resemble a stained glass window.

You can also use glass paints to create stencilled or freehand designs on any glass surface, so giving your glazing projects a distinct and individual touch.

Cleaning glass

If it is to remain an attractive addition to your home, glass must be cleaned regularly. Grease, nicotine and condensation can build up to a surface film which is extremely hard to shift. Regular washing with a household detergent or proprietary window-cleaning product is the only way to keep your glass in sparkling condition.

Right: *A beautifully etched design adds individual character to this fixed glass partition screen in the kitchen. Similar effects can be achieved more easily using glass paints*

Michael Nicholson/EWA

Flat roof repairs

● **Tracing leaks** ● **Repairing felted roofs** ● **Types of metal-clad roof** ● **Repairing and renewing metal-clad roofs** ● **Repairing rotten boarding** ● **Dealing with rotten structural timbers** ● **Alternative coverings to metal**

A. *Modern materials and working methods have put major flat roof repairs well within the scope of the competent DIY enthusiast. The stepped roof shown here (originally zinc) has been covered with a polymer bitumen compound melted on to a felt underlay*

A flat roof is built in much the same way as a timber floor. Its joists, which also act as rafters, can run either across the roof or from front to back – normally, whichever way is shorter. On top of the joists is a continuous decking or sarking, its boards laid at right-angles to the joists, of either square-edged or tongued-and-grooved boarding. And on top of that is the roof covering, which can be of bitumenized or metal compound.

Where such a roof differs from a floor is that it must have a fall from back to front for rainwater run-off. Sometimes the joists themselves are fixed 'to slope' to provide this; more often, sloping strips called firring pieces are provided – one on top of each joist if these run from front to back, or just one at each side if the joists run crosswise.

At the ends of the rafters, two main types of finish are used. In one type, the joist ends are trimmed flush with the wall below and fascias cover the gap between joists and wall. In the other, the joist ends project 150mm or 200mm beyond the wall and are trimmed with fascias at the ends and soffit linings underneath. Short stub rafters project over the side walls.

Tracing the leak
The first sign of a leak in a flat roof is usually a discoloured damp patch which appears on the ceiling or the walls below. This may not be directly below the leak, because water can penetrate the roof covering, run down a joist or across a ceiling and produce a stain a couple of metres away from where it entered. So, wherever the dampness appears, inspect the whole roof before you begin any repairs or order materials.

Dampness beneath a flat roof can also be caused by condensation, which may show up as discoloured patches or mould growth across all or part of the ceiling. Unfortunately there is no way of identifying the cause without dismantling the roof covering and the boarding below it.

Working on a flat roof
Several types of compound (see below) are available for roofing work. They are not necessarily interchangeable, so either use the type recommended or ask the advice of your builder's merchant.

If possible carry out any re-roofing work in warm weather. This makes roofing compounds easier to spread and with felt roofs lessens the chance that the felt will later stretch and form bubbles.

Before you begin recovering any roof, make sure you have on hand a sheet of heavy-duty polyethelene. This will help keep the room below dry should you discover that the roof decking or joists are rotten and in need of replacement.

Repairing the flashing
Damaged flashing is a frequent (and easily repaired) cause of leaks, so inspect it first. But do not start any repair work if further inspection shows that the roof surface needs replacing, or if you intend to add wood wool insulation slabs in which case the flashing will have to be inserted at a higher level. (See also pages 1364 to 1368.)

Masonry buildings: The flashing is mortared into the brickwork about 150mm (two brick courses) above the roof surface. If it is damaged, replace it with a new strip. If not, use a hammer and cold chisel to remove the loose or cracked mortar to a depth of about 50mm from the wall surface. Wedge the flashing into this opening with small pieces of brick, and fill the joint with a stiff mortar (four parts of sand to one of cement) leaving it for two days to set.

At the bottom, if there are gaps between a flashing strip and the roof surface, gently lift the flashing by running a decorator's stripping knife beneath it. Apply a thick coat of rubberized roofing compound and press the flashing back into place, weighting it down with a row of bricks until the compound 'goes off'.

Timber-framed buildings: The top edge of the flashing is tucked under a weatherboard (clapboard) about 100mm above the roof surface, and nailed through the weatherboard behind it to the supporting studs. If the flashing is damaged, lift the weatherboard which covers it by prising it from the bottom with a crowbar. This will also loosen one or more boards above. When you have lifted the board enough to get access to the fixing nails, punch the nail heads right through the old flashing with a nail punch (nail set).

Nail on a new piece of flashing and

re-nail the loosened weatherboards, replacing any cracked boards while you are at it. Where the flashing extends over the roof covering, repair it in the same way as you would a masonry building.

Bitumenized felt roofs

Bitumenized roofing felt, unless carefully maintained, has a shorter life than other types of roof covering. For this reason strict regulations or local ordinances control its use, and sometimes ban it.

On garages and other outbuildings, a single layer of roofing felt is adequate, and is accepted by most authorities. On houses, if the use of felt is permitted at all, two or three layers are usually insisted upon. In the UK, for example, the building regulations specify that such roofs must have at least two layers of roofing felt, bonded both to the roof and to each other, and that the felt in each layer must have a minimum weight of 13kg per 10m². The top layer of felt must be covered in mineral chippings of about 2mm size, bedded in bitumen.

Roofing felt tends to wrinkle or bubble if laid direct from the roll. So, if you are using large pieces for repairs, or relaying a whole 'skin', cut off the lengths you will need and leave them unrolled for two or three days before using them. (This is another reason for working in warm weather.)

Repairing felted roofs

On buildings with a single-skin roof, such as garages, it is not worthwhile spending a lot of time trying to patch or seal a damaged roof. Roofing felt is relatively cheap, so it is easier to strip off the old lot and renew it. However, two or three layer roofs are worth repairing if they show only minor damage.

Basic maintenance: Felt will last longer if it is painted every three or four years with a purpose-made renewing compound, such as Aquaseal Water-proofing roof paint. First sweep off any loose chippings, then apply the compound with an old brush working from the high side of the roof towards the low side.

Fine cracks: Fine cracks can be filled by painting the whole roof surface with a bitumen-latex compound such as Syntha-pruf or Aquaseal No. 40 Waterproofer. Do use an old paintbrush, however, because it will be impossible to clean this off afterwards.

Blisters: If the top layer (only) of the roof shows an occasional small blister, you can repair this in much the same way you would a blister in wallpaper. Being careful not to cut into the lower felt layers, score an X across the blister. Gently lift the resulting triangles then, with a putty knife or paint scraper, work in a generous layer of roofing mastic (roof

1 A typical stepped, zinc-covered flat roof long overdue for recovering. Roofs like this must be stripped completely as the timbers may be rotten

3 On this roof, removal of the zinc reveals patches of rotten sarking. The affected boards must be replaced and the joists below checked for rot

cement) such as Aquaseal Mastic. Using flat-headed galvanized nails, refix the cut pieces. Finally, across the top, fix a patch big enough to cover the repaired area plus 40mm or so all round. Stick this down with roof mastic and nail all the edges with closely-spaced (25mm centres) galvanized flatheads.

Patches: If the damage extends over a large area – up to about 300mm square– you can repair it with a double patch. First cut from new felt a patch big enough to cover the damaged area. Lay this on the roof and use it as a template while you mark out the area to be removed. Then, cutting through the top layer of felt only, remove the damaged bit by cutting it out with a handyman's knife and lifting it gently with a paint scraper.

Spread roof mastic generously into the hole, roll the patch into place so that no air is trapped beneath it, and nail it

2 Removing the old covering, flashing and joint rolls is largely a matter of brute force, but take care when you are lowering the debris to the ground

4 Once the flashing has gone, rake out three or four courses of mortar joints on the parapet walls to provide a key for the new rendering

5 It is nearly always economic–and often necessary–to remove the existing guttering and fascia. Work from scaffolding if at all possible

Repairs and renovations

6 Prime the back of the new fascia board before offering it up to the roof. Screw it firmly to the joist ends then prime the face and edges

7 The lead flashing strip can now be fitted. Arrange for it to overlap the fascia completely then nail it to the sarking with galvanized clouts

8 Use a piece of batten as a 'dolly' to dress the lead flashing down over the fascia. Again, this job is best done working from a scaffold tower

9 The final part of the fascia work involves nailing a primed length of batten over the flashing to give its lower edge a suitably sloping profile

10 Roll out the first length of felt underlay across the roof at the fascia end. Allow plenty of overlap at the edge and against the parapet walls

11 With a second length overlapping the first, begin securing the felt using 19mm galvanized clouts spaced at 75mm centres. Use extra at the overlap

around the edges. Now cut another, bigger patch and apply it over the first one as described above.

Replacing felted roofs

Roofing nails on a felted roof will lift more quickly if you use a crowbar and hammer, hammering the crowbar through the felt and under the nails.

To strip the old felt, warm it with a blowlamp in one hand while you cut and tear off the felt with the other. The warmth will help free any stubborn mastic, but do not overdo it or you will set fire to the old roof.

With the old felt stripped off, scrape off any ridges or bumps in the old adhesive with a paint scraper.

The method of relaying a felted roof is described on pages 1252 to 1256. But before you do this, inspect and if necessary replace any unsound timber as described below.

Metal-clad roofs

Three types of metal cladding – lead, zinc and galvanized sheet steel – are commonly used on flat roofs. Copper is also used occasionally (but rarely on houses).

The roof structure underneath is basically the same – joists and a timber roof decking – as for bitumenized felt. There are, however, some important detail differences:

Underlay: To prevent condensation forming on the cold underside of the metal and dripping into the ceiling cavity, an underlay of felt or waterproof building paper is laid between the deck and the metal.

Longitudinal joints: Because of expansion and contraction due to changes in air temperature, rigid joints in sheet metal – welds, for example – would cause the roof to buckle and/or its fastenings to tear themselves loose. So joints which are longitudinal – that is, running in the same direction as the fall of the roof – are formed over wood rolls; these allow for expansion but are high enough to prevent water penetration. The profiles of the rolls and the ways in which the metal is dressed over them, vary according to the cladding used. Figs B to G give some of the most commonly used examples.

Cross joints: Wood rolls could not, of course, be used for joints running at right-angles to the roof slope, or puddles would form. Galvanized sheet steel presents no problems in the sizes used for housing. But for lead, copper and zinc, small steps – called *drips* – are formed across the roof at intervals of between 2m and 3m, depending on the metal. At each drip, the edge of the sheet on the lower level is turned upwards to form a lip of between 50mm and 75mm. The edge of the upper sheet is then turned down over this lip.

George Wright

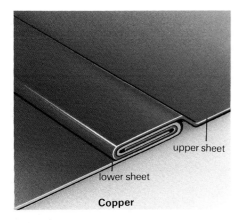

Copper

B. *Joints between copper sheets which run across the fall must be folded as shown if they are to remain watertight. The roof slopes from right to left*

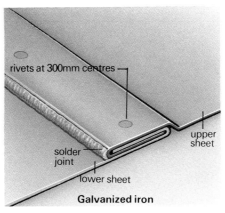

Galvanized iron

C. *A similar, but simpler, fold pattern is employed for galvanized steel sheet. In this case the joint is riveted and the gap between sheets soldered up*

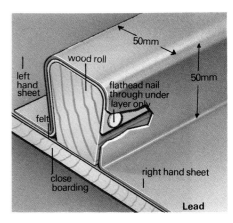

Lead

D. *A joint between lead sheets made with the fall. The left hand sheet is nailed to the wood roll and the right hand one dressed over it to hide the gap*

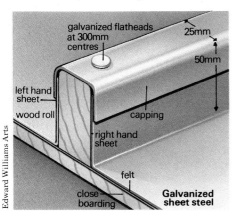

Galvanized sheet steel

E. *The same joint made with galvanized steel sheet. The sheets are dressed to near the top of the wood-roll and a capping piece then riveted over them*

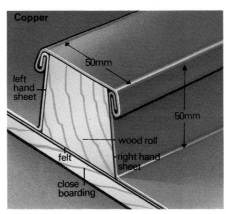

Copper

F. *On a copper roof, the roll capping pieces have to be made up and folded over the edges of the adjoining sheets as shown – an intricate, laborious job*

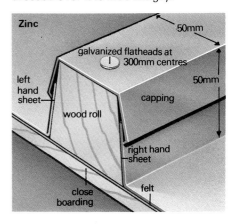

Zinc

G. *Roll joints between zinc sheets are much the same as for galvanized steel sheet – using purpose-made capping – but the rolls have a different profile*

Repairing and renewing metal

On metal roofs, cracks and corrosion are most likely to occur where the metal has been folded to form joints.

If the cracks are tiny and the corrosion has not penetrated the sheet, you can paint the entire roof surface with a liquid bitumen roof proofer (such as Aquaseal No. 5) using an old brush. (This will give a black roof surface, so do not do it if the colour is unacceptable.)

More serious damage cannot be satisfactorily patched: you have to lift and replace the damaged sheets or resurface the entire roof.

If you do have to replace one or more sheets, examine the joints carefully as you prise them apart so that you can duplicate them when you instal the new sheet. The basic joints are shown in figs B to G, but there are many variations. For example, where the metal at the ends of the wood rolls is dressed over a step or where a roof meets a boxed-in gutter.

With a copper or lead roof, try to leave intact the securing strips which are fastened under the wood jointing rolls as this may prevent your having to remove and renew the rolls. As with a felted roof, you should examine – and if necessary renew – any roof timbers before relaying the roof.

The basic methods of forming 'dry' joints in sheet metal are on pages 2138 to 2144. But for this job you will need to make extra-long joints, so something like an adjustable work bench and two long bars over which to bend the metal are virtual necessities.

There are a number of points to bear in mind when dealing with lead, galvanized steel, copper and zinc.

Lead: Lead is easy to lay and to dress, but expands and contracts rapidly with changes in temperature. Over a period of time this causes it to 'creep' down the roof, so it is normally fixed only in small sheets

H. *Longitudinal or roll joints are always made with the fall. The cross joints made across or against the fall are designed not to trap water*

– up to 1.5m². To avoid having too many steps in the roof, this usually means 2m from front to back and 900mm between wood rolls.

Standard sheet sizes in the UK are 6m × 2.4m and 6m × 1.2m. Before you buy measure carefully the pieces you will need, remembering to allow for upstands; lead is too expensive to waste.

When laying, note that nails are used

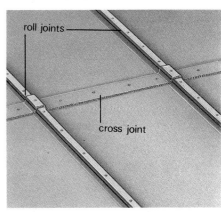

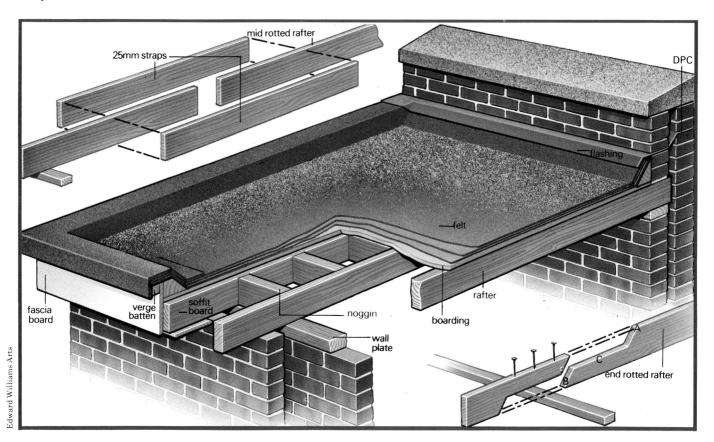

25mm straps — *mid rotted rafter* — *DPC* — *flashing* — *felt* — *rafter* — *fascia board* — *verge batten* — *soffit board* — *noggin* — *boarding* — *wall plate* — *end rotted rafter*

Edward Williams Arts

only where they will be covered by another sheet of lead dressed over the top. No sheet is nailed on opposites sides, in case contraction tears the sheet from the nails. This means that, for example, a sheet which serves as the underlay at one wood roll must serve as the overlay at the next roll and only the underlay is nailed.

For dressing, do not use steel tools which could cut through the lead. A wooden mallet is best.

Galvanized steel: Galvanized sheet steel, much used in Australasia, is also reasonably easy to cut, lay and dress, normally requiring only simple right-hand bends. Only where cross joints are needed on a long roof is it necessary to fold, rivet and solder as shown in fig. C.

Do not nail galvanized steel to the roof decking itself, but only around the lower edges of the fascias. At each wood roll, the upturned edges of the sheets are secured with a capping piece which is fastened with galvanized flatheads.

Copper: Copper is difficult to handle unless you are an experienced metal-worker, because it requires precisely-made folded joints. Large scale repairs are therefore best left to professionals.

Zinc: Zinc is also difficult to handle, being brittle and easily broken when folding. But because it comes in larger sizes than copper – in the UK 2.4m × 900mm – it does not require folded joints between the roof steps.

Like other sheet materials, zinc should

never be nailed to the roof decking. It is held in place by clips which, like those for copper, are fixed under the wood rolls and turned up and over to catch the edges of the sheets. A purpose-made capping piece covers the cut edges (fig G).

Repairing the boarding

With the roof covering removed, inspect the roof decking (sarking). Any rotten boards (test by probing with a knife point) must be replaced. If the boards run transversely (at right-angles to the fall), any cupped boards will act as water traps and may even cut through the surface – especially if this is lead or felt. Lift the cupped boards and turn them over, bow sides upwards, before re-nailing.

Also lift a board or two at the perimeter of the roof to check that the joists, fascias and so on are sound. This is also an opportunity to check whether the roof has been insulated and, if not, to do something about it. The heat loss (or gain, in hot climates) through an uninsulated flat roof is considerable.

The techniques for lifting and replacing roof decks are exactly the same as for a suspended floor (see pages 182 to 187 for further details).

Dealing with rotten joists

The ceiling joists in a flat roof are unlikely to suffer damage unless the roofing has been seriously neglected. However, you may strike problems.

I. *A typical flat roof construction and two methods of dealing with rafters affected by wet rot, depending on whether the damage is at the end or the middle*

● If you find signs of rot, establish whether it is wet or dry rot (see pages 492 to 495). Dry rot must, in this case, be dealt with by professionals although it is rarely found in flat roof timbers.

● Try to remove or replace any rotten timber without disturbing the ceiling below – otherwise you will have another major repair job on your hands.

● If you have to cut away a section of wet rot, always cut away enough material so that there is no chance of the rot recurring. A dark patch on the 'good' side of the cut, even if it looks and feels solid, is a warning sign of incipient rot and means you should remove more wood – preferably 1m past the visible damage.

● All existing timber in a roof in which you have found wet rot should be given a generous coat of clear wood preservative, such as Cuprinol Clear, to prolong its life. Pay particular attention to the end grain.

● When you reassemble the roof, protect all end grain – for example, the ends of the fascias and the ends of the joists where they abut on to fascias – with a good thick coat of wood primer. This is not often done in the UK, where the timber available used to be of good quality; but with the porous soft woods in use today it is essential.

Rotten ends

In a roof with overhanging joists (fig. I) the ends of the joists sometimes contract wet rot. There are two ways of dealing with this, depending on the extent of the damage.

• If only one or two of the joists are damaged, you can cut a new section of joist and join it to the old with a stepped scarf joint (fig. I). The joint should be over–or at least within a few centimetres of–the wallplate.

To make the joint you cut the first sloping step (A in the diagram), then sever the joist at B. Cutting the horizontal line C is awkward when joists are closely spaced, but it must be done accurately. So set the depth required on a marking gauge, mark both sides of the joist, and rip-saw alternately from either side to make sure that the saw does not dip below the line. With the final cut C made, you can hold the new length of joist against the old while you mark it to fit. A small packing piece will be needed at the wallplate if your new timber is narrower than the old.

• If most of the ends are damaged, the easiest way to deal with them is to saw off the overhang and use a flush, instead of overhanging, finish. First remove the gutter, soffit, soffit supports and fascia.

Rotten firring pieces

Firring pieces on the tops of joists are usually nailed, but not glued, and can easily be removed for replacement with new ones. If several are rotten, check with your timber merchant before you start measuring and cutting new ones–it may be much easier, and probably no more expensive, to use a whole new set.

Rotten edge joists

If a joist at the edge of the roof is damaged, you again have two choices:

• If the wet rot is mainly along the top edge, split the joist lengthwise and replace the top half. To remove the rotten half, you will need a circular (rotary) power saw with its width gauge suitably set. With the new top pieces cut, join the two with urea formaldehyde adhesive and with No. 10 or No. 12 woodscrews long enough to penetrate the top strip and two-thirds of the way through the old bottom strip. Insert the screws at 300mm centres for full strength.

• Replace the complete joist. This is the only method that works satisfactorily if the joist is badly rotten, but is almost impossible to do without damaging the ceiling below.

If the ceiling is plasterboard (wallboard), you could try lifting the joist from one end only and a few millimetres at a time. In this case get a helper to watch where indentations start to appear

12 *Before you felt over the step in the roof, nail lengths of triangular section timber against it to smooth the slope. Prime the wood thoroughly*

14 *Render the raked-out brickwork just above the fillets with a stiff mix of 1:3 mortar. When dry, coat both the render and the fillets with primer*

16 *With the backing peeled off and the length rolled up half way, melt the underside using a propane torch and press it on to the roof*

13 *Once a length of felt has been fully nailed, nail primed lengths of triangular fillet over the top of it at the junctions with parapet walls*

15 *You can now cover the roof with polymer bitumen compound. Start by laying out the first length with an overlap at the fascia and trim it to fit*

17 *When you have completed one side of a length, melt and roll out the other. The underside is ready for bonding when it starts to bubble*

George Wright

Repairs and renovations

18 *When the main roof area is covered deal with the edge overlap. Melt the underside with the torch then press the flap over the flashing*

19 *The flashing at the parapet walls is made using 450mm strips of the polymer bitumen compound. Simply melt it and dress it over the fillets*

20 *The final job is to point the area just above the flashing strips. Give the mortar a sloping finish so that rain cannot get behind the strips*

on the ceiling – indicating nail positions – and drive the nails right through the plasterboard.

If the ceiling is lath and plaster, you could try cutting the joists into short lengths about 300mm long, and then tap each piece from side to side until its works itself free. Afterwards nip off the ends of the protruding lath nails.

If you do succeed in freeing the joist in this way, do not attempt to nail the ceiling to the new joist when this is installed. Instead, nail strips of hessian across the top of the joist and let them hang down the side and 'trail' on to the ceiling. Damp the hessian, wood and ceiling with a 4:1 mixture of water and PVA adhesive, and use plaster of paris, bonding plaster or a proprietary cellulose filler to make an adhesive 'strap' over the new joist.

Alternatives to metal cladding

If a metal-clad roof is badly damaged over its entire area and looks to be in need of renewal, there may be an easier and cheaper (though not as longlasting) alternative to fresh sheet metal. Such a material is glass fibre reinforced polymer bitumen compound, sold in the UK under the brand name Torchtite Supa 35 in rolls 7m × 1m. The compound is laid in a single layer over an asbestos felt base and is bonded to the surface by melting the backing with a propane torch. It has been used successfully on the Continent and in the UK for the last 12 years and is thought to have a life expectancy of 10 to 20 years depending on the prevailing weather conditions. However, you should check whether it is acceptable to your local building control office before finally deciding to use the treatment.

The first stage of the job is to strip the roof of the existing sheet covering, together with all the old flashing, cappings and jointing rolls.

Follow by making a thorough inspection of the sarking and, if this shows signs of rot, the roof timbers below. Renew or patch as necessary and replace fascias and soffits at the same time. Prime all new timber thoroughly.

Where parapet walls are present, prepare them for rerendering by raking out the mortar joints for three or four courses. If you have fitted a new fascia, obtain a suitable flashing strip to cover it and overlap the sarking by about 50mm (metal is still best for this). Nail the strip to the sarking with 19mm galvanised clouts then fold and dress it over the fascia as shown in fig. 8. Follow by nailing a suitably primed length of 50mm × 25mm battening along the top of the fascia (fig. 9) so that the flashing slopes into what will later be the guttering.

Now prepare the base using a suitable asbestos felt (such as BS2B in the UK). Start at the lowest point of the roof (the fascia end) and work across it at right-angles to the fall. Unroll the first length of felt so that it follows the edge of the fascia and secure it with 19mm galvanized clouts at 75mm centres. The felt should reach right to any parapet walls.

Repeat the procedure for subsequent lengths, working up the roof and using fillets to 'smooth' any steps (fig. 12). Overlap by 75mm between lengths, with the overlaps in the direction of the fall. When all the felt is down, nail suitably primed triangular section wood fillets at the junctions of the roof and parapet walls then trim the felt down to these. Now is the time to re-render the parapet walls above the fillets. When the render is dry, prime both it and the timber with spirit-based bitumen primer.

To apply the polymer bitumen compound you will need to hire a heavy duty propane torch with gas bottles. Tell your hire shop dealer what you intend to use it for and he should be able to advise you on a suitable model. Do not make the mistake of hiring a model that has an insufficient capacity.

Like the felting you start laying the compound at the fascia end, but this time with a 50mm overlap to dress over the board itself. Unroll the first length of the compound – being sure to wear heavy duty heat-proof gloves – and trim it to fit around any obstructions. Then roll it half way up again, removing the polyethylene backing as you do so.

Taking the torch, and standing behind the roll, play it over the whole of the underside of the compound for a length of about 150mm until it melts. Then roll this section forward and press it down with your feet on to the felt. Continue this melting/rolling pressing procedure until the first half of the length is laid, then roll up and lay the other half in the same way. At the fascia, heat up the underside of the overlap and simply press it down over the flashing (fig. 18).

Repeat the entire procedure for the next and all subsequent lengths, working up the roof until it is covered and overlapping between lengths by 75mm. Avoid treading on the compound until it has completely cooled and bonded to the felt or you may damage the material that has just been laid on the roof.

When the roof itself is complete, cut 450mm strips of the polymer bitumen compound for the flashings. Melt the back of each strip with the torch and press it into the parapet wall junction, dressing it over the filleting as you do so. Again work from the fascia end up the roof, so that all overlaps are with the fall. Finish by pointing above the strips (fig. 20).

Making drawers

● **Drawer materials** ● **Two types of runner** ● **Cleat hung drawers** ● **Drawer fronts** ● **The design features of drawer carcases** ● **Essential tolerances** ● **Making multiple drawer units** ● **Assembly and fitting hints**

Drawers for cabinet and fitted furniture can be made up in any one of a number of different ways, and the choice is even wider when it comes to finish and installation. Nevertheless there are some cardinal rules about drawer making which it is useful to know and these hold true both for simple structures and for work of a finer nature.

Figs B to M show twelve standard variations of drawer design—including proprietary kit-built models—and give constructional details. Below are some of the points to consider before finalizing your design, together with a few hints on assembly and installation.

Materials

For the sides and backs of most drawers, plywood is the best material. It gives maximum strength for minimum thickness and thus wastes as little space as possible. It is also less liable to bow than solid timber, and less vulnerable to destruction than the cheaper types of man-made board such as chipboard.

Do not, however, use plywood in a situation where one of its cut edges will slide on another piece of wood. This is because, however you cut it, at least one ply will have its end grain rubbing against the adjoining surface, and it is virtually impossible to cut the end grain absolutely smooth. Examples of how to get around the problem are given below.

Cleats and kickers (see below) are best made of hardwood, metal or hard plastic, depending on where they are used. Do not use softwood for cleats except on small drawers carrying light loads, for example clothing. Wooden cleats are usually 17mm deep and 12mm thick. Drawer bottoms are often made of 3mm hardboard, but plywood is less apt to bow.

Runners

The type of runners used, and the way they fit into the outside carcase, are the most important factors in designing drawer units. Drawers can be supported in two ways.

Bottom hung: Bottom hung drawers sit on a rail which runs across the front of the

carcase, flush with its vertical members (fig. F). Behind this rail running fore and aft are other horizontal members, called *kickers,* across which the bottom of the drawer slides. Rails and kickers are also needed at the top of a cabinet to prevent

the top drawer from tipping forwards.

Remember that rails and kickers reduce the depth of the space available for drawers in any given cabinet. To calculate how deep the drawers should be, you must allow for one more rail than there will be drawers and divide the remaining depth accordingly.

Bottom hung drawers must be

A Below: *A well fitting, attractive and efficiently running drawer is an essential complement to any piece of furniture of which it is a part*

Ray Duns

precisely made and dead square otherwise there is a danger of their jamming against the sides of the carcase, or of an ugly wide crack appearing between the carcase and drawer front. To conceal this gap, the fronts are sometimes made oversailed (fig. F). In this case the bottom of one drawer and the top of the drawer below will overlap the rail between them by a few millimetres. Leave a gap of at least 2mm between them at this point to avoid one drawer grating on the other.

Bottom hung drawers also need two drawer stops—one at each side—to prevent them from being pushed too far into the cabinet. These are usually made of plywood, glued and pinned to the rail.

Cleat hung drawers: These are suspended on wooden, metal or plastic strips, which can be attached to, or set into, the side of the drawer or the side of the carcase (figs C, D and H). These strips are concealed by extensions of the drawer front (in a four-piece drawer) or by a false front (in a five-piece drawer).

Cleat systems reduce the width available for drawers in a given cabinet. To calculate how wide the drawers will be, you take the width between carcase sides and deduct the width of the cleat system.

Cleat hung drawers do not need drawer stops, this function being fulfilled by the drawer front hitting the end of the cleat. This means, however, that the front edge of the cleats must be set at a very precise distance from the front edge of the carcase to prevent the drawer from protruding or receding. This is usually done by scribing a line down the inside of the carcase, parallel with the front edge, before the carcase is assembled.

Where a drawer is oversailed, this step

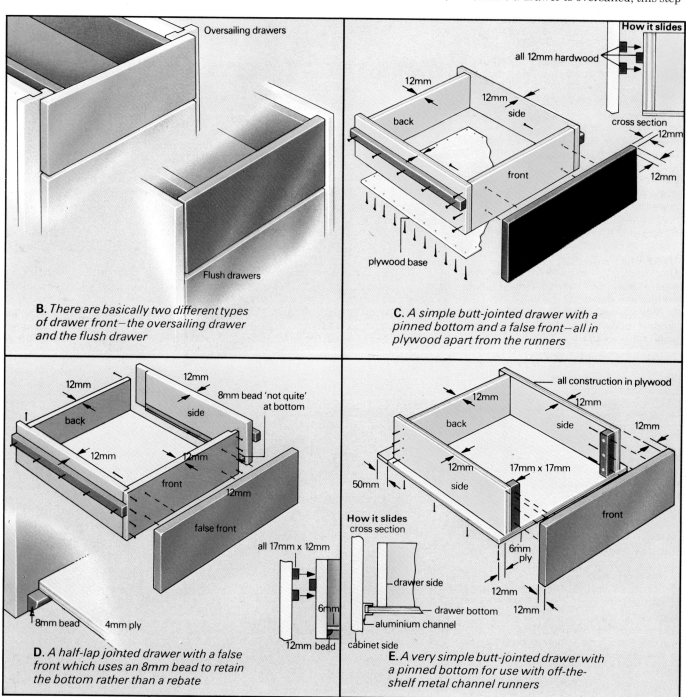

B. *There are basically two different types of drawer front—the oversailing drawer and the flush drawer*

C. *A simple butt-jointed drawer with a pinned bottom and a false front—all in plywood apart from the runners*

D. *A half-lap jointed drawer with a false front which uses an 8mm bead to retain the bottom rather than a rebate*

E. *A very simple butt-jointed drawer with a pinned bottom for use with off-the-shelf metal channel runners*

1 *One easy way to made drawers is to use a plastic profile section kit. These come complete with the PVC profile and corner clips, ready for assembly*

2 *Cut the profile to the correct length then hammer the corner clips firmly into position using a resin bonded adhesive for extra strength*

3 *When three sides are fixed into a square U shape, slide in the base board (3mm white faced hardboard or plywood) and add the fourth side*

is of course unnecessary because the cleats run to the outside edge of the carcase on both sides.

In other respects, cleat hung drawers do not need to be made with quite the same precision as bottom hung drawers since the 'fit'—or lack of it—between cleat and drawer is invisible. So most modern factory-made drawers use this system.

Drawer fronts

Drawer fronts can be either of two types—flush or oversailed—and both designs are shown in fig. B.

They do not affect the design of the carcase itself (except the top, which must project far enough to cover them) unless drawers with a wide lip or oversail are wanted on a carcase built of narrow components. But they do affect the use, and placing, of cleats and drawer stops. With oversailed doors, for example, the cleats come right to the front edge so you do not need to decide what type of fronts you want before you begin building your drawers or drawer kits.

Carcase design

Carcase and drawer design go hand in hand. Unless you are fitting an extra drawer or drawers into an existing carcase—in which case you must do the best you can with what you have got—you should design your carcase and drawers simultaneously.

Carcases may be boxed or framed, both of which are described in details on pages 824 to 830 and 869 to 874.

The box carcase, built up of solid slabs, can accept drawers of any kind but can also be enormously wasteful of material. When you are installing a bottom hung drawer, for example, it uses a whole shelf for support when only a rail and two kickers would do.

Frame carcases, on the other hand, are more economical but sometimes do not provide adequate support—for example a cleat hung drawer the cleats of which are supported only at the ends is likely to sag in the middle. A useful compromise from

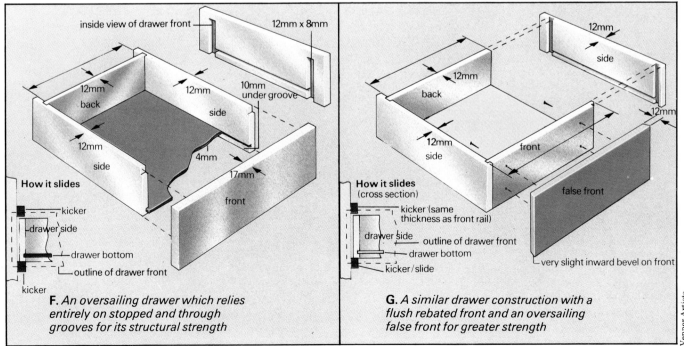

F. *An oversailing drawer which relies entirely on stopped and through grooves for its structural strength*

inside view of drawer front — 12mm x 8mm
12mm back — 12mm side — 10mm under groove
12mm side — 4mm — 17mm — front

How it slides
kicker
drawer side
drawer bottom
outline of drawer front
kicker

G. *A similar drawer construction with a flush rebated front and an oversailing false front for greater strength*

12mm side
12mm back — 12mm front
12mm side — 12mm
false front

How it slides (cross section)
kicker (same thickness as front rail)
drawer side — outline of drawer front
drawer bottom
kicker/slide
very slight inward bevel on front

Venner Artists

4 *Place the drawer on its runners and measure the distance between the top of the cupboard or drawer below and top edge of the drawer*

5 *Transfer the measurement to the front timber and cut it out, then fix it to the drawer by screwing through the false front with suitable screws*

6 *The plastic profile drawer kit is extremely flexible and since the design includes a false front, it can be made to match any existing furniture*

which to begin designing is a carcase whose upright members or partitions are solid, but whose horizontal members are strips. Cleats or kickers can be screwed to the solid uprights, or better, screwed right through the upright into the cleat on the other side. Rails can be set into the uprights by means of stopped housing joints or pinned and glued.

Whichever type of carcase you choose, allow a small margin of at least 25mm between the backs of the drawers and the carcase into which they are going.

Tolerances

Drawers must be made slightly smaller than the openings into which they fit cr they will swell and jam in damp weather. For bottom hung drawers, a space of 1mm at each side and 1-1.5mm at the top is perfectly adequate.

For cleat hung drawers, these tolerances are reversed: at the side, allow 1.5mm between each cleat and the surface against which it will bear; above the cleat, to prevent a rocking motion which would wear it, try to restrict the clearance to 1mm or so. This means that cleats must be set against a steel rule and pulled straight as they are fixed in place.

Multiple drawers

When making a multi-drawered unit, especially using power tools, it may save time to cut similar components in batches. But in assembly, treat each drawer and its position in the carcase as a separate operation. When you are satisfied with the fit, number the drawer so you know where it goes.

If drawers in the same unit have to be of varying heights, always put the deepest drawer at the bottom. In fact, most drawer units look better if their drawers are of graded sizes.

Assembly hints

Always assemble drawers on a dead flat surface, such as a laminate-finished worktop. If they show any sign of twisting out of shape, lay a sheet of flat material

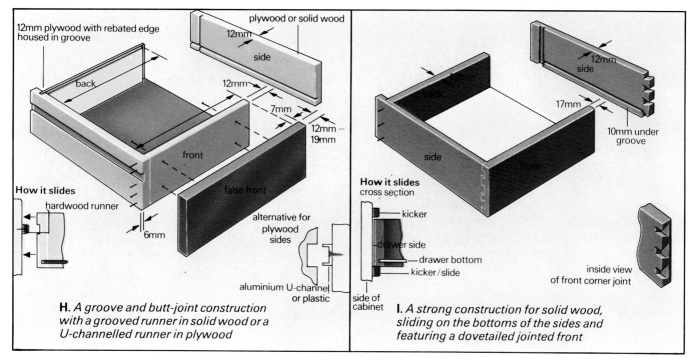

H. *A groove and butt-joint construction with a grooved runner in solid wood or a U-channelled runner in plywood*

I. *A strong construction for solid wood, sliding on the bottoms of the sides and featuring a dovetailed jointed front*

over them and weigh them down until the adhesive hardens.

At the same time, check constantly that the assembled drawers are in square. An error here will mean either that the assembled drawer will not run properly or that one side of the drawer front will protrude or recede.

When making 'five piece' drawers — those with a front and a false front — always assemble the basic drawer and fit it into the carcase before marking and cutting the false front. This gives you the opportunity to make tiny adjustments to

the spacing or alignment of the latter if this should prove necessary.

Also, try to arrange the timber for false fronts in the most attractive pattern. For example, two or more doors which sit side-by-side are best 'covered' by the same length of timber cut into pieces.

Fitting cleats and runners

Cleat positions should if possible be marked on the sides of the carcase, using a precise tool such as a marking knife, before carcase assembly begins. When you come to fix on the cleats, begin by

screwing them in place without adhesive. Check that the drawer slides freely before fixing the cleats permanently — first the awkward right-hand side (if you are right-handed) then the more accessible left-hand side.

If components have to be fixed to both the drawer and carcase, as with three-cleat systems and proprietary tracks, fix the carcase components first unless the manufacturer's instructions direct otherwise. If adjustments are necessary, it is easier to make them on the drawer than in the cramped space of the carcase.

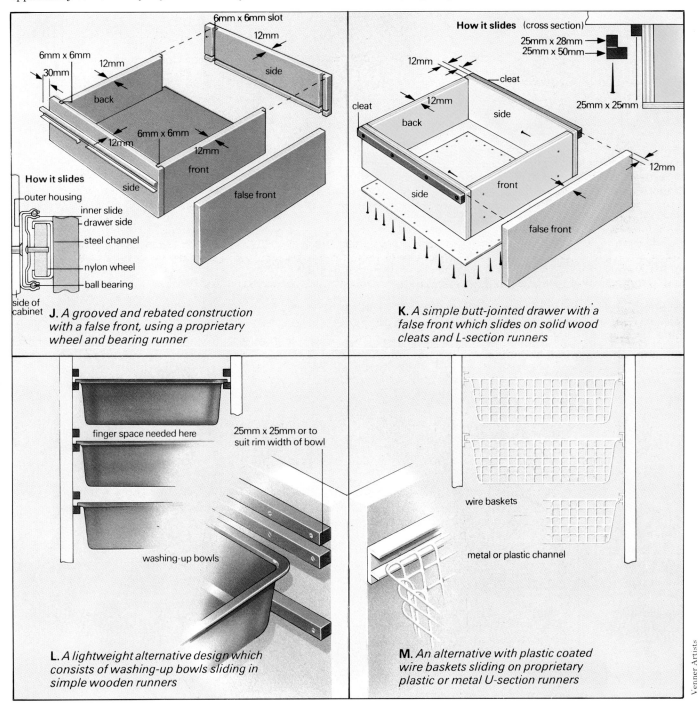

J. *A grooved and rebated construction with a false front, using a proprietary wheel and bearing runner*

K. *A simple butt-jointed drawer with a false front which slides on solid wood cleats and L-section runners*

L. *A lightweight alternative design which consists of washing-up bowls sliding in simple wooden runners*

M. *An alternative with plastic coated wire baskets sliding on proprietary plastic or metal U-section runners*

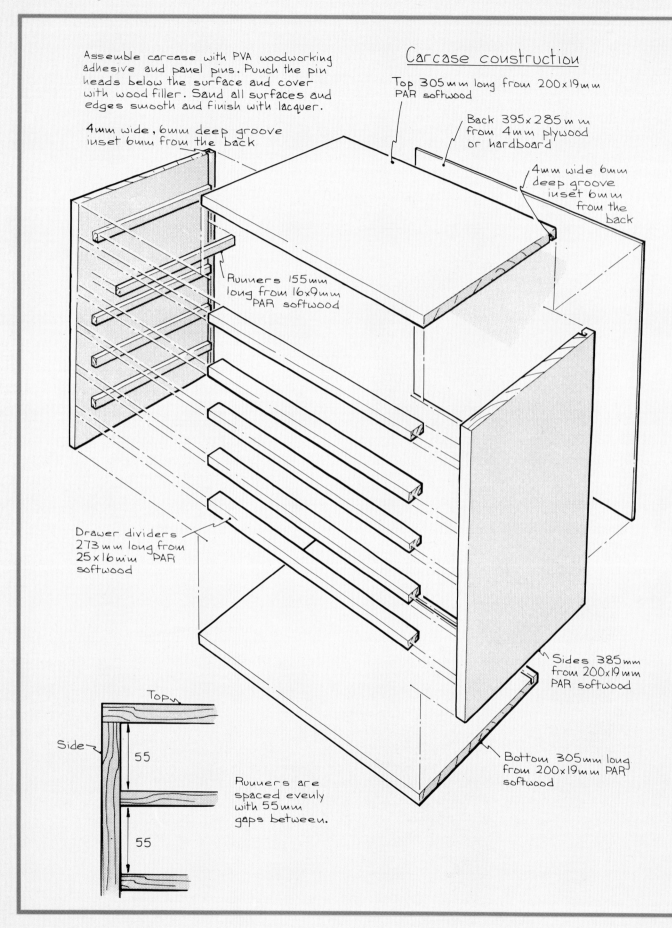

Assemble carcase with PVA woodworking adhesive and panel pins. Punch the pin heads below the surface and cover with wood filler. Sand all surfaces and edges smooth and finish with lacquer.

4mm wide, 6mm deep groove inset 6mm from the back

Carcase construction

Top 305mm long from 200x19mm PAR softwood

Back 395x285mm from 4mm plywood or hardboard

4mm wide 6mm deep groove inset 6mm from the back

Runners 155mm long from 16x9mm PAR softwood

Drawer dividers 273mm long from 25x16mm PAR softwood

Top

Side

55

55

Runners are spaced evenly with 55mm gaps between.

Sides 385mm from 200x19mm PAR softwood

Bottom 305mm long from 200x19mm PAR softwood

Drawer construction

Assemble with PVA woodworking adhesive and panel pins. Punch the pin heads below the surface and cover with wood filler. Sand all surfaces and edges smooth. Finish the interior and front with lacquer, and wax the outside of the sides to aid smooth running.

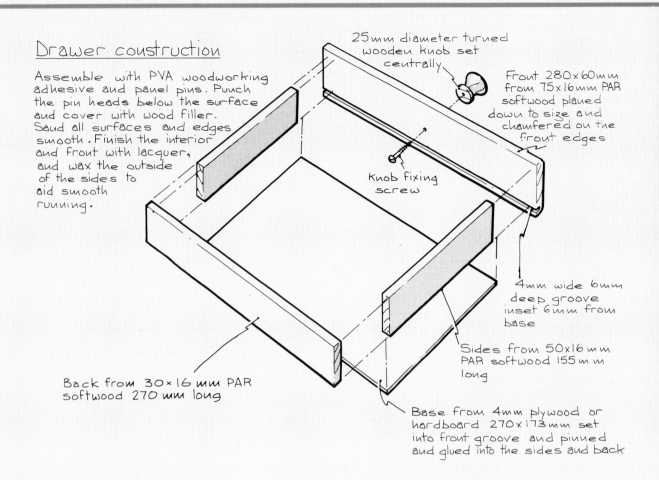

25mm diameter turned wooden knob set centrally

Front 280 × 60mm from 75 × 16mm PAR softwood planed down to size and chamfered on the front edges

Knob fixing screw

4mm wide 6mm deep groove inset 6mm from base

Sides from 50 × 16mm PAR softwood 155mm long

Back from 30 × 16mm PAR softwood 270mm long

Base from 4mm plywood or hardboard 270 × 173mm set into front groove and pinned and glued into the sides and back

A small chest of drawers

This miniature chest of drawers is sure to find plenty of use around the home. Use it for storing sewing threads and accessories, jewellery, or just those easily-lost wood-screws.

Most of the construction is in softwood, so you can leave it plain or finish with stain or paint to suit different uses. The drawer bases are in hardboard—or preferably thin plywood as it will slide better— and are small enough to make from offcuts.

Cut out the boards from the carcase, attach the runners and glue and pin together, slotting the back into a groove. If this is difficult to cut, make the back 12mm smaller and support it on 6mm square battens. Add the drawer dividers, pinned and glued between the sides. Punch the pin heads below the surface and cover with matching filler.

All the drawers are identical and are assembled with glue and pins. Fit the bases into a groove in the front or support them on battens as above. Add knobs of your choice.

Antonia Toma

Kitchen redesign – 3

The decision-making process ● Tackling the jobs in the correct order ● Two conversions of a galley kitchen ● Working out the core area of the kitchen ● Alternatives for a larger kitchen ● Drawing up working plans properly

Armed with all the information supplied in the first two parts of this series, you should now be ready to plan and start work on your own kitchen. The order of deciding on the design is quite different from the order of work (see the panels below). Full instructions on drawing up scale plans are given in part 1 of the Home improvements course (see pages 2033 to 2039) but special advice for kitchen plans is included below.

However, as you may now be feeling confused by the options open and where to begin, this last part of the series begins by

A. Below: *The kitchen that was the base for conversions A and B. Very little thought had gone into its layout and basic considerations such as worktop height and the core triangle seem never to have crossed the planner's mind*

following through how two kitchens were remodelled, giving alternative plans for two very different households in each case. Although you can never find the perfect solution to your own kitchen by copying another, analysing the design and renovation processes can be both instructive and inspiring.

The small kitchen

First consider a kitchen as inconvenient and antiquated as anyone is likely to have to tackle. It measures only 3m × 1.85m and has a single frosted window overlooking the neighbour's wall. Two doors at either end open inwards, one directly on to steps down to the garden and the other into a hallway with a small larder. It is typical of kitchens in semi-detached two storey houses built in the UK in the 1920's, though it has plenty in

common with – and many of the same problems as – small kitchens throughout the world (fig. A).

For all its limitations even this kitchen can be modified to serve either a young couple on a very tight budget or a large family with many bulky appliances to accommodate and the money to make necessary changes.

Conversion A

Fig A shows the kitchen the young couple took over. An array of antiquated fitments were lined up against the window wall: a miniature dresser and old stove at one end, a scratched enamel sink and drainer served by an erratic gas water heater at the other. A fridge had taken up the gap, plugged by a long flex into a single socket high up by the internal door. The opposite wall had a high shelf and radiant electric fire fixed to it; against it was a table used for eating despite the doors. The garden door had wet rot and the window wall streamed with condensation during cooking because it was brick faced with thick plaster and shiny paint. The floor was surfaced with cold tiles in bad condition.

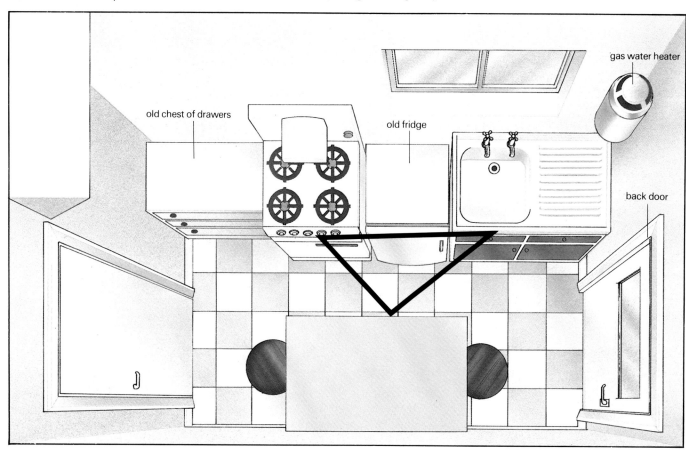

old chest of drawers

old fridge

gas water heater

back door

Steve Cross

Considerations: The couple had to use the larder for household storage so all food, crockery and utensils had to be found places in the new kitchen. This was not a major problem as they shopped regularly and kept few bulk items. However, they had to house their giant washing machine in the kitchen and also wanted to eat breakfast there.

As their finances were limited, they could not spare cash for insulation or ventilation at this stage. Their carpentry skills were also limited so any alterations had to be simple. Consequently their design had to incorporate off-the-shelf kitchen fitments and secondhand appliances wherever possible. Unfortunately the only item they could retain was the radiant fire as everything else was either too worn, or wasted valuable space.

The couple's solution: Nevertheless, by careful planning they were able to make a neat bank of fitments along the window wall forming the core area of the kitchen (fig. B). This was the only place for a smooth, long run of work surfaces. As it was exactly 3000mm and their self-assembly tops and units came in

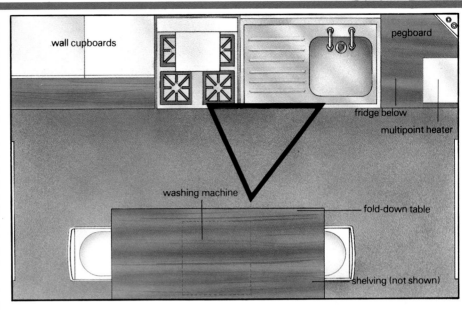

B. Above: *A plan view of conversion A as carried out by a young couple on a limited budget. With a little thought they have created a core area along one side with more setting-down space*

C. Below: *Conversion A carried out on a galley kitchen by a young couple with a limited budget. This view shows the core area with all the major appliances ranged along the outside wall*

D. Above: *Looking in the opposite direction you can see the multipoint gas heater and the glass-paned outside door*

E. Below: *This view shows the folding breakfast table/worktop, with the washing machine removed for clarity*

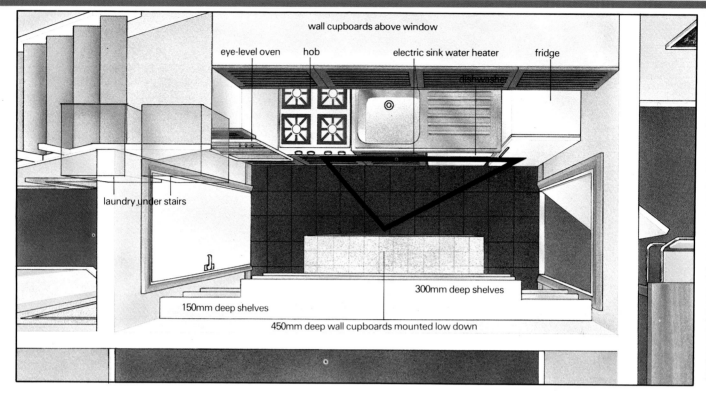

wall cupboards above window

eye-level oven hob electric sink water heater fridge

dishwasher

laundry under stairs

300mm deep shelves

150mm deep shelves

450mm deep wall cupboards mounted low down

F. Conversion B: a plan for the same galley kitchen but now with a dining room added on at the back. The laundry is now under the stairs leaving more room for food preparation, storage, and an automatic dishwasher

multiples of 500mm, they decided to buy a cooker and fridge less than 500mm wide to give maximum worktop space. Even so, to allow for clearance space on both sides of the stove and fridge, they had to remove the skirting boards either side of the run of units.

The run in conversion A is formed by two 1000mm knock-down base units with space between for the cooker and a gap by the garden door for the fridge. One unit is topped by a stainless steel sink and drainer, the other has a wall cupboard over it and gives a spacious surface con- veniently near to the cooker. Another 500mm of work surface is created by fixing a worktop with battens screwed to the garden wall and sink unit over the fridge. Above it a pegboard with hooks gives vertical storage for frequently used pots, pans and utensils.

More work surfaces are provided on the other wall by fixing a standard 1500mm × 600mm worktop on folding brackets. This also serves as a breakfast bar and storage area for the washing machine. When the latter is wheeled to the sink for use, the worktop is folded down to allow access to the fridge and garden.

Rehanging the inner door gives more space for eating—stools are pushed under the worktop at other times. The swing of the garden door could not easily be changed because of the steps, but the door itself is replaced by an off-the-shelf glass panelled door, double glazed for warmth and fitted with a roller blind. The wall above the breakfast bar is covered with adjustable shelves to house the crockery. The radiant heater is mounted on brackets to clear the shelves beneath.

It can be seen that this arrangement required minimal alteration to services. The waste for the new sink was easily connected to the yard gulley as only the position of the drainer was changed. A new gas multipoint water heater with balanced flue replaced the old heater and this also serves the bathroom upstairs. Connections were taken from the cooker's gas pipe and mains water to the sink, brought up in the corner of the worktop and boxed in discreetly.

More electric power points were installed—a double one above the longer worktop for small appliances and another by the garden door for the fridge and washing machine. The single socket by the internal door was replaced by a double one to serve the radiant fire and other appliances.

Note that decoration in the conversion is kept simple and natural—the colour dictated by the new blue and white vinyl flooring. The base units are left white and 'wood effect' laminate is chosen for all work surfaces. The walls are painted with white 'anti-condensation' paint and this makes the room bright enough to be lit adequately by two pendent lights taken from the central ceiling rose. Bright colour is restricted to lampshades, stools covers and plants on the window.

The works
1. Order new appliances, fitments or taps; delay further work until arrival
2. Strip out old plumbing (gas, hot and cold water); waste pipes; electric wiring; loose plaster; obsolete fitments and appliances
3. Instal new electrics—socket outlets; other power outlets; lighting outlets and switches (but not light fittings)
4. Renew or repair surfaces to ceiling, walls or floors but do not paint yet
5. Fit all new appliances
6. Fix all new fitments, including worktops over appliances
7. Decorate ceiling and walls—paint, tiles, paper
8. Decorate old and new fitments
9. Lay new floor covering
10. Fit new light fittings
11. Put in loose equipment and furniture

Conversion B

Costs and structural alterations do not always have to be kept to an absolute minimum as they were in conversion A. With wider scope, and by making full use of the available wall space, the same small kitchen can be converted to serve a family of five (Fig. F).

Limitations: In this case the kitchen improvements were part of extensive alterations to the house. A dining room extension was built outside the garden door so that this could be rehung to swing outwards. The family planned to eat in the living room next to the kitchen, so a hatch was knocked between the two. Central heating was installed, with the gas-fired boiler being positioned in the living room fireplace.

The kitchen had to accommodate an electric wall oven, gas hob, dish washer and a large fridge–plus generous storage for bulk provisions and lots of crockery and utensils. The larder was not available as it had to be converted into a laundry room to take a washing machine and dryer (achieved by putting a vent in the external wall).

The solution: A close look at the conversion shows all the appliances ranged along the window wall: the tall fridge by the garden door with a mechanical air extractor above it, the wall oven built-in with cupboards above and below at the opposite end. Between the two is a 1800mm worktop with the gas hob and a stainless steel sink set into it. Beneath are the dishwasher and a small

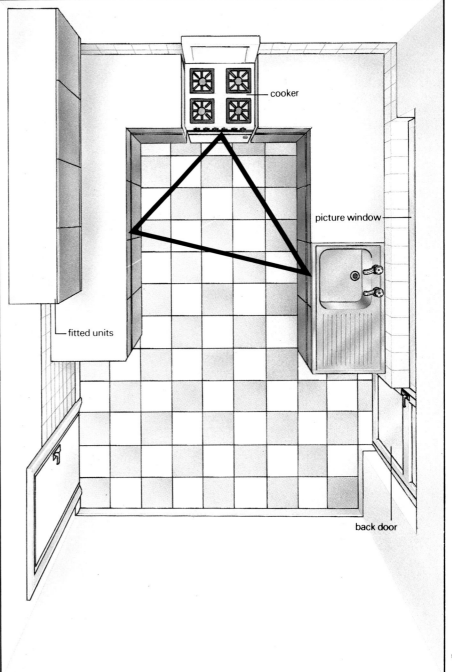

cooker

picture window

fitted units

back door

Steve Cross

G. This fitted kitchen in a new house under-utilizes the space available, and is inflexible in its layout. In many households a complete redesign of the kitchen area would be necessary in order to make it conform with the requirements of the average family

electric hot water heater–installed for economy as the boiler and main hot water tank are positioned so far away from the kitchen sink.

Purpose-built melamine faced shelving between the dishwasher and under-oven cupboards stores bulky items in everyday use. Things which are needed less frequently can be stored at high level on the 600mm wide length of melamine faced blockboard spanning the entire wall above window level. All the shelves and cupboards on this wall are fronted with louvred doors to streamline the rather complex arrangement. A 100mm removable plinth is fitted in front of everything except the fridge, and both the fridge and dishwasher are on castors for easy cleaning. Even the centre wall spaces are utilized: a cooker hood over the hob; a pegboard between oven and window for utensils; and glass shelves across the window for plants.

The opposite wall—except the spaces for the hatch and central heating radiator—is also put to good use, but only for storage and work surfaces. The main work surface—fixed to the wall by brackets—is cut from a standard 2000mm × 450mm worktop; this allows for the maximum possible length between the radiator and a flap-down table by the garden door. Adjustable shelving covers the top half of the wall in various depths, and three cupboards are fixed directly to the wall below the worktop.

Drainage in this conversion had to be changed considerably. The dishwasher waste was plumbed into the sink waste at the top and both were then connected to the existing gulley. The washing machine waste could not easily run along the external wall to the gulley because of a soil vent pipe. So it was taken in 38mm plastic pipe low along the inside wall before discharging into the gulley. Cold water taken off the mains supply to the sink supplies both machines. Water for the small electric heater below the sink was also taken off the mains supply—a special dual-flow sink mixer tap allows for this arrangement.

Many extra socket outlets were needed. The 30 amp outlet for the wall oven and cooker hood switch were put on the side of the oven housing. A double socket outlet for the water heater and dish washer was installed under the sink, with another pair for the fridge and mechanical air extractor by the garden door. Two pairs of socket outlets for small appliances were put over the long worktop, beside the serving hatch. Lighting was restricted to overhead pendent lights.

Again, decor is simple but cheerful; the ceilings and walls (including the pegboard wall covering) are painted white and all joinery, including the plinth and skirting board, is dark green. The work surfaces, window reveal and splashback are all tiled in a green and white pattern to match and the floor is cork tiles over tongued-and-grooved chipboard. Brightly coloured lampshades provide contrast.

Conversion B is very compact, yet it is not oppressive to work in because of the plentiful natural light from the window and glazed glass door—and also because this door and the hatch give a feeling of space extending beyond the kitchen. The excellent ventilation makes the room more comfortable and the semi open-plan storage aids accessibility. The work surface area is large enough for family meals and despite the tight galley shape it is safe for the cook to have helpers because sink and hob are close at hand.

Larger kitchens

Some kitchens do not have such a tight restriction on space but nevertheless need remodelling to make them more workable. This can even be true of a brand new room like the U shaped fitted kitchen shown in fig G which is very wasteful of the available space.

H. *Conversion C as carried out by a family who wanted to eat in their kitchen and had to keep several appliances to hand as well. Theirs is now a traditional larder/laundry/dining kitchen*

Conversion C

Fig H shows the way a family who wanted to eat in the kitchen—and house a large fridge, a dishwasher, and a washing machine and dryer—made the room suit their needs. The sink and cooker locations remain unchanged but half the U is removed. One 500mm wall cupboard is left between window and cooker but all other units have been banished to elsewhere in the house; new storage space can also be created by installing narrow shelving on adjustable brackets above the dining area.

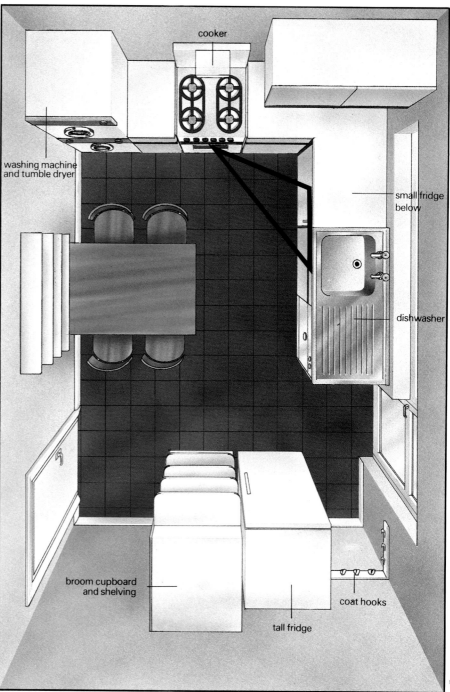

cooker

washing machine and tumble dryer

small fridge below

dishwasher

broom cupboard and shelving

tall fridge

coat hooks

Steve Cross

As the table is large—1200 × 800mm—and a maximum of 800mm from the perimeter worktops, it also serves as a sit-down work surface and laying out space. The empty space next to the cooker is filled by an off-the-shelf floor cupboard and by the washing machine with the dryer mounted above. As this is an external wall, the dryer vent can be let into it and the washing machine waste plumbed via a 'clearing eye' to the gulley serving the kitchen sink.

Some of the base units on the sink wall have been removed to house the dishwasher—plumbed into the sink waste—and a very small fridge. This was bought because the old, giant fridge had to be on the far side of the room and so used more as a larder. Shelving bolted to the adjacent broom closet takes food en route to the fridge. The area by the back door is reserved for coats and dirty shoes.

I. *Conversion D: a more functional layout with food preparation and laundry areas carefully separated. This is a less homely kitchen designed purely for speed and efficiency in every task*

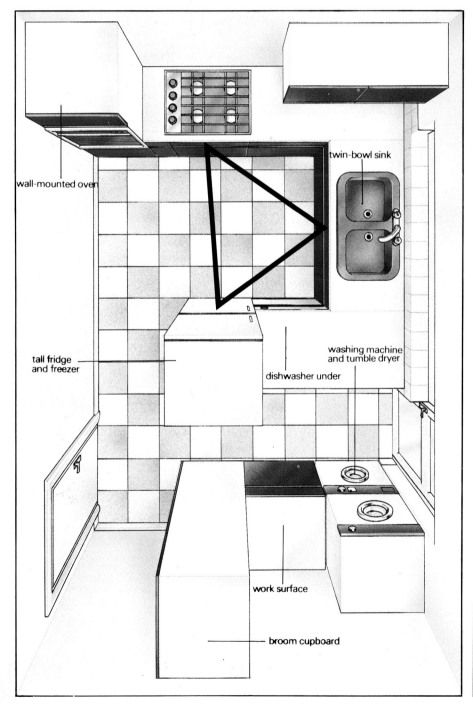

wall-mounted oven

twin-bowl sink

tall fridge and freezer

dishwasher under

washing machine and tumble dryer

work surface

broom cupboard

Conversion D

The same basic kitchen can also be very successfully modified so that laundry and food areas are kept completely separate and quite different appliances included in the layout (fig. I).

In this case the washing machine with dryer above is located by the garden door with a worktop for sorting clothes beside them. The same leg of the U is demolished as in conversion C, but some worktops are re-used to form a peninsula dividing the kitchen zones with a fridge freezer at the end. This gives a neat 'core' triangle between the hob and the double sink which replaces the original sink and drainer. The dishwasher is fitted under the peninsula worktop and the wall oven is installed in the far corner, separated from the hob by 300mm of setting down space with storage below.

Drawing up plans

General instructions for drawing up plans were given in the first part of the Home improvements course (see pages 2033 to 2039) but for a complex room like the kitchen it is worth drawing a 1:20 plan using the 1:20 section of a metric scale. Also it is better to use tracing paper so that you can make a separate plan later for the room's permanent fixtures and use moveable cut-outs for shifting other fitments and appliances to various possible locations.

If you use tracing paper you will have to make your own grid. Mark it off at 300mm intervals from the 1:20 metric scale. Begin your drawing in the corner of the kitchen and start measuring where the lines of the grid meet. As the floor and elevation plans will be complicated, it may be easier to make freehand sketches first and put measurements on to these.

Be prepared to measure at several levels to include wall fixtures and power supplies—both for the floor plan and elevations. Fitments obscuring corners should be shown in section on elevation plans. Include information about drainage outside too as this is important when considering changing the positions of 'wet' appliances.

When you have settled on your new layout and checked that you can buy any new fitments and appliances in the sizes you want, draw up a final set of plans—floor and elevations—and consult the two 'action' panels for an exact timetable.

Warning
In certain countries such as Australia and New Zealand all plumbing and electrical installation work must be entrusted to the relevant licensed qualified tradesman by law.

Unusual floor coverings

Floorcoverings play an important role in any room in the house. And while carpet might be the most popular choice for many people, there are other ways of covering the floor to produce an unusual and decorative surface

For many people these days, fitted carpet seems to be the rule for most, if not every, room in the house. There are times, however, when an alternative floorcovering might be worth considering – whether for practical or purely financial reasons. Fitted carpets may have many advantages over other types of floorcovering, but using something different in just one or two rooms can add a touch of individuality and variety to your home. Fortunately, there is plenty of choice.

Coir and rush matting

Coir and rush matting provide a good alternative to carpet with many of the same advantages, including warmth and quiet, but at a much lower cost. The natural colours and attractive weaves blend well with most styles of interior decoration and are especially appropriate in rooms furnished with natural woods.

Coir is made from coconut fibre and is usually handwoven. It is available in broadloom (about 4m wide), in strips and as individual mats. Broadloom coir may be backed with latex to give extra durability and softness. This backing is essential if you are fitting the matting wall to wall as it helps to keep the coir flat and prevents dust from becoming trapped underneath. Coir is relatively simple to lay but should be cut about 10-20mm oversize and left for about 24 hours to settle before trimming to fit. Secure the edges firmly with tape or carpet adhesive.

Broadloom coir is suitable for use in any room where you would use a carpet but like all natural fibres it absorbs water, so is not such a good choice for the bathroom or kitchen. And because it cannot be scrubbed, it is not entirely hygenic for kitchen use. Otherwise, coir is relatively easy to maintain. Dust and grit can be removed with a vacuum cleaner and stains with warm, soapy water.

Strips of coir matting are very cheap and easily adaptable for use in a hall or

Below left: *Coir matting laid wall to wall makes an ideal low cost floor covering and its neutral colours suit even the most stylish surroundings*

Below: *Rush mat 'tiles' sewn together are another inexpensive covering. They work particularly well when used to add warmth and relief to a bare floor*

Brigitte Baert

Brecht-Einzig Ltd

Michael Nicholson/EWA

tough finish. It is not essential to apply undercoat, but this may be helpful if you plan to use a light colour.

Unlike varnish, the choice of colours available is virtually unlimited. You might simply paint the floor the same colour as other woodwork in the room to give a feeling of spaciousness or perhaps choose a darker shade of the main colour, or one which complements it. A matching ceiling and floor can be very striking in a large room, especially if curtains and other accessories also match. Black or deep glossy red adds drama to the decor, and looks particularly striking with contrasting white rugs scattered over the floor to add warmth underfoot.

Stencilled and patterned floors

A painted floor allows you to give full rein to your creative instincts. If you have a steady hand and an artistic eye you might try painting your own freehand designs over the surface. But even without any special skills, you can still achieve really exciting and unusual effects with just a

Transworld Feature Syndicate

awkwardly shaped room. The strips are about 910mm wide and can be sewn together using strong twine. The lengths are easily cut with a sharp knife and the raw edges can be bound with jute binding tape to prevent fraying. Coir strips are not usually backed with latex.

Individual mats offer a very wide range of weaves, shapes, sizes and textures. They are particularly striking when used in combination with sanded and varnished floorboards and are also most effective on tiled floors.

Besides coir, various types of grasses and rushes are used for mats, some of which are very hardwearing. Rush is particularly tough: the mats are usually made from plaited rushes woven into patterned 'tiles' and then sewn together. Seagrass mats are made in a similar way and are also durable. Both types are suitable for use in any room, including the kitchen and bathroom, and are easily taken up and shaken or cleaned with a vacuum cleaner.

Split reed mats from China are rather more delicate and are best used in a bedroom or sitting room. They have a slight sheen and may be woven in quite intricate patterns, sometimes incorporating coloured stripes.

Painted floors

Stripped and varnished floorboards have become fairly commonplace during recent years, but painted floorboards are still quite unusual and can form a most attractive design feature.

The basic technique is the same—the boards must be sanded smooth, holes and rough edges repaired and then several thin coats of paint carefully applied. A good quality gloss paint provides a spectacularly shiny and surprisingly

Transworld Feature Syndicate

Above: *Using decorative borders—in this case stencilled patterns—does a lot to brighten what might otherwise be a rather plain expanse of floor*

Left: *The painting concept can be taken a stage further by adding stencils and more colour. In this example the stunning effect belies its low cost*

line of the floorboards. In the first case, paint the base colour and allow it to dry completely before adding the stripes. Mark out the pattern with masking tape and again, using non-drip gloss, apply one colour stripe at a time.

The technique for stripes along the floorboards is slightly different. Select three or four close shades of the same colour—perhaps coding them A, B, C and D. Then, having thoroughly prepared the floorboards, use chalk to lightly mark each board across the entire room with the appropriate colour code. Paint all the shade A boards first and allow them to dry before using shade B and so on.

Apply several coats of each shade, making sure that you use the same number of coats for each colour. This treatment is particularly striking where the floorboards are narrow or where there is a long vista, such as in a hall.

Rubber stud flooring

Synthetic rubber stud flooring is a relatively new covering in domestic applications but it is exceptionally well suited to modern decor. Waterproof and extremely durable, it is suitable for any room in the house and its flexibility makes it ideal for staircases and for raised or sunken areas. The studs have a cushioning effect, making the flooring non-slip and unusually comfortable underfoot. It is therefore ideally suited to use in a bathroom or child's playroom. It is easily washed using warm soapy water and maintain an attractive shine despite constant wear and tear.

Rubber stud flooring comes in a range of colours and patterns and although it is rather expensive, the cost is counter-balanced by the fact that it is almost

little care and patience.

One possibility is to stencil a border around the edge of the floor. This can be a simple pattern in a single colour or more elaborate using several different colours. Either buy a stencil from a crafts shop or make your own from strong cardboard. A particularly effective idea is to trace off a feature from the wallpaper to use as a pattern for the stencil.

Paint the floorboards first, allowing plenty of time between coats. Leave the final coat for 48 hours before beginning the stencil. Measure the position for your border and mark the corners and key points lightly with chalk. Start from the centre of one edge and work outwards.

A non-drip paint is easiest to use and you should apply all of one colour, allowing it to dry completely, before applying any second or third colours. You may find it helpful to use masking tape to keep the stencil absolutely straight and accurately positioned while you work.

There are, of course, numerous other ways of using stencils apart from a continuous repeating border. For example, you could paint a decorative pattern in each corner of the room or even a central design feigning a 'rug'.

Painted stripes are cheap and easy to do and produce a highly decorative finish. These can form a pattern around or across the room, or can run along the natural

Above: *Synthetic rubber is a tried and tested industrial floorcovering but is only just beginning to find widespread favour in domestic applications*

Below: *In the kitchen, synthetic rubber competes well with the more traditional floorcoverings—in terms both of its resiliency and its warmth underfoot*

indestructible. It does require some skill to fit, however, and even though manufacturers usually supply full instructions, it may be worth having it laid professionally to obtain a really sleek finish which does it justice.

Wood floors

'Traditional wood flooring is not only practical but also very beautiful. It looks elegant in virtually any room, though in the bathroom and kitchen where spilt water may make it slippery it is probably not such a practical choice. Laying floor blocks or strip flooring is quite a major project and requires some DIY experience and expertise. However, an equally attractive effect can be achieved more easily and with less upheaval using mosaic panels.

These panels consist of small tongues of hardwood bonded in a basket weave pattern to a fabric backing. They can be laid directly on to clean, level floorboards or on to a solid floor, using much the same technique as you would for cork tiles.

The panels, which are usually 290mm or 460mm square, are pre-sanded and should be laid with a spirit-based or bitumen adhesive. When the adhesive has dried, the surface should be sealed with either several coats of lacquer or an application of shellac button polish followed by several coats of wax polish (follow the manufacturers' recommendations for suitable products). When completed, the effect is virtually indistinguishable from traditional wood block parquet.

Brecht-Einzig Ltd.

Above: *Wood strip flooring gives a clean and natural look to any decorative scheme and the softwood shown here is comparatively inexpensive*

Below: *Mosaic wood panels are by far the easiest to lay of all wood floor-coverings, yet they can look just as effective as conventional blocks*

Camera Press

Concreting tools

● **Machines and tools to make concreting easy** ●
How to break up old concrete rafts and screeds ●
Compacting machines ● **Types of concrete mixer**
● **Choosing a mixer** ● **Using and maintaining a
mixer** ● **General safety precautions**

As well as the smaller power tools – drills, saws, routers – which get regular use and are therefore worth buying, a wide range of larger tools is now becoming available for hire at specialist shops. These take the hard slog out of many heavier DIY jobs and the hire charges are often very cheap when compared to the amount of time and effort saved in the process.

This part of the course deals specifically with machines to help mix and lay concrete – often the most backbreaking of all DIY tasks. The next part looks at what other large tools can be hired – anything from wallpaper strippers to space heaters and carpet cleaners.

Concrete breaking

Quite often you need to break up and remove a poorly laid concrete screed in order to re-lay it properly or clear the ground ready for some other use. One way of doing this is by hand, using a sharp cold chisel and a heavy club hammer, but this would take a long time and might even be impossible in some instances.

One alternative is to use an ordinary power drill fitted with a large masonry bit to make a series of random holes at roughly 50mm intervals in the screed: on thin screeds this should weaken the structure enough to make it a lot easier to break up by hand. For tougher screeds (20-100mm thick) you could buy or hire a heavy-duty industrial drill fitted with a large diameter bit (see page 1606).

A. *There are plenty of tools available for hire to take the hard slog out of larger concreting jobs. A barrow type mixer like this is particularly useful*

1 *Heavy duty industrial jack hammers like this are supplied with a range of interchangeable heads, enabling you to use them for breaking or drilling*

2 *One of the most obvious uses for the jack hammer is in breaking up an old or badly laid screed. Keep the broken pieces for use as hardcore*

3 *Levelling off the site and picking out old roots and boulders is one concreting job that must still be done by hand – at least initially*

Jon Bouchier

4 *Fortunately, plate tamping machines like this are available to help with the final levelling. They also compact the ground to form a solid base*

5 *Having pegged up the site and constructed suitable formwork, you can prepare the base as necessary. Here hardcore from the old screed is laid*

6 *The larger chunks of hardcore can be broken up with the jack hammer but you will probably find it just as easy to smash them with a sledge hammer*

But for really rapid concrete breaking there is no tool to compete with a jack hammer and small electrically-powered models suitable for DIY use can be hired fairly easily (fig. 1). At first sight, jack hammers look rather like large industrial drills; but instead of being fitted with a bit they have a number of interchangeable 'heads', some of which are pointed, others spade-shaped rather like a cold chisel. The breaker has a vibrating up-and-down action and can force its way through practically any depth of concrete in a relatively short time.

When using a jack hammer, be sure to wear a pair of stout shoes with protective toecaps. Work systematically from one side of the screed to the other, breaking off sizeable chunks which can easily be

disposed of. Push the whole machine down so that the head is forced into the concrete then, once you have broken through, pull back on the handles to loosen each chunk (fig. 2).

When the whole area has been broken up in this way the lumps can be loaded on to a wheelbarrow for disposal. You can then prepare the site as you wish. If you plan to lay a new screed, the sub-base should be thoroughly flattened first and all large rocks and vegetation removed.

Compacting machines

A compactor is a machine which flattens and consolidates hardcore and rubble bases prior to concrete pouring (fig. 7). By hand this usually takes a great deal of time and effort, so buying or hiring a

compactor is well worthwhile – especially if you have a large area to cover.

The ideal compactor for home use is the type with a vibrating plate. This can be rolled across the site rather like a wheelbarrow while the plate vibrates and imparts a series of blows to the area directly underneath. It is usually unnecessary to go over the site more than two or three times to flatten it completely. Once this has been done you can prepare the area for concreting by erecting formwork (see pages 272 to 277).

Concrete mixers

For jobs requiring only a small amount of mortar or concrete it obviously makes sense to mix by hand. But larger projects where a great deal of concrete is needed can be greatly speeded up by the use of a concrete mixer.

The most suitable mixer for domestic use is the *barrow* type. This consists of a cylindrical drum (where the mixing takes place) mounted on two pneumatic or solid rubber wheels. At the rear of the mixing drum are two handles enabling the whole machine to be trundled around and tipped rather like a wheelbarrow (fig. C).

The main advantage of the barrow mixer is that it is relatively small and light, meaning that it is easy to transport in the back of a van or estate car to wherever it is needed. And once on site, you simply push it to the most convenient spot for mixing. If you are filling a footing, for example, you can move the mixer right up to the edge of the trench and deposit the mix without having to transfer it using a wheelbarrow (fig. 18).

The second type of mixer is much larger and cannot be moved around as easily as the lightweight barrow type. It consists of

B. *The ideal concreting site should have everything set out neatly, within easy reach. Where the formwork is above the surrounding ground, provide ramps for your wheelbarrow or mixer and take extra care when dumping a load*

a fixed H-frame mounted on four wheels which carries the mixing drum (fig. C). The whole body of such a machine obviously cannot be tipped up on end when loading and unloading the drum. Instead, a large wheel mounted on the body of the mixer enables the drum to be turned to either side and a separate locking device allows you to lock it to any position (fig. C).

For many DIY jobs larger mixers can be too cumbersome: they are very difficult to move around without the assistance of at least two other people and can only be transported to the site by being towed behind a vehicle. However, on really large buildings jobs–such as building an extension–their greater capacity makes them practically the only type worth hiring.

Choosing a mixer

One of the first things to look for in a concrete mixer is load size. This tells you how much material (sand, cement, ballast and water) it can accommodate at one time.

The capacities of concrete mixers are described in various ways–sometimes as the volume of *dry* ingredients and sometimes the volume of *mixed* concrete

7 *With the hardcore in more or less regularly sized pieces, you can use the plate tamper again to level and compact them into the ground*

that can be handled in one go. Usually both figures are given, so a mixer described as having a capacity of 140/100 is able to hold 140 litres of dry ingredients and 100 litres of concrete. When choosing a mixer do not be fooled by the size of the rest of its component parts; concentrate

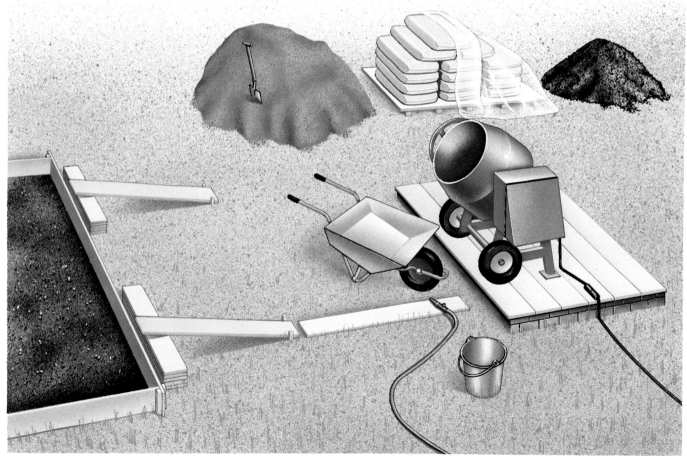

Bernard Fallon

8 *Wheelbarrow type concrete mixers may be electric or petrol driven and are useful for transporting cement or ballast as well as for mixing*

9 *If the mixer is to stay in one place, use the stand provided or a platform of timber and bricks to bring it up to a convenient working height*

10 *If you have never used a concrete mixer before, use a bucket to help measure out the cement and ballast in their correct ratios*

11 *Later, as you get more experienced, you can shovel the ingredients straight into the mixing drum, taking care not to spill any on site*

12 *Lay bags of cement on a sheet of hardboard or polyethylene – this will protect them from moisture and make cleaning up easier*

13 *On your first load, shovel in half the aggregate and then add half the mixing water. Let them combine for a few seconds before adding all the cement*

Jon Bouchier

instead on the capacity. A mixer with a capacity of 140/100 should be large enough to deal with most DIY projects.

Treat capacities as nominal only. The exact volume of materials you can safely load into a drum will vary considerably depending on the type of cement, sand and other materials you are using – and you can only really discover this for yourself by using the machine.

Next, have a look at the type of motor installed. The smaller wheelbarrow type usually have either petrol or electric motors while the larger four wheeled models are invariably petrol driven. Electric motors are quiet and give few starting problems compared to the petrol variety. But because they have a long lead stretching from a nearby electrical

socket outlet to the machine you must be constantly on guard against accidents (see below).

If you want to consider getting a barrow type mixer, try to choose one that is easy to handle and tip – remembering that it will be full of concrete when you do so. The best mixers have a safety bar at the front end to stop the machine getting out of control while it is tipped.

Some manufacturers and hire shops make a small stand which raises the machine off the ground so that is it high enough to be tipped into a wheelbarrow. And on some models this stand allows the mixer to be swivelled through 360°, which can be very useful if you are working in a confined space or want to load the drum from one side and

discharge from the other. If you cannot find a stand which is suitable, stand the mixer on a patch of ground slightly higher than the rest of the site or build a small platform of bricks and boards so that you can tip it more easily (fig. B).

Using a mixer

Mixing dry ingredients and moving load after load of wet concrete is not easy, even with a machine. Your first consideration should be to plan the layout of your site with this in mind, so reducing the amount of shovel work and travelling you need to do at any one time.

If you have sand and aggregate delivered in bulk, shovel these into neat piles on one side of the mixer so they can be loaded easily. You can keep the materials from getting soiled by placing a number of large clean boards on the ground and then loading the sand and aggregate on to them when it arrives at the site (fig. B).

Have another flat and clean area nearby where you can split open bags of cement and transfer them to the mixer. Remember that the cement should be covered overnight with tarpaulin or sheets of polyethylene in case of rain.

Lay on a supply of water by fixing a garden hose to the nearest tap. This might mean a lot of water splashing around while you are mixing but it avoids having to constantly refill buckets from the tap. If you can fix a device to the end of the hose enabling you to turn it off on site so much the better. In the absence of a convenient tap aim to use a large clean drum from which you can scoop buckets of water. If you intend transporting the mix in a wheelbarrow, make sure that you can get the barrow under the mouth of the tilted mixing drum. Build a platform if necessary (see above).

If you decide to tip the mixed concrete straight on to the ground prior to shovelling it into a wheelbarrow or directly into the formwork you have prepared, lay sheets of plywood beneath and around the mixer. This ensures that the concrete does not get mixed up with earth and stones, and also makes the site easier to clean up afterwards.

It is surprisingly easy to lose control of a wheelbarrow laden with heavy concrete, but the chances of you doing so can be reduced by providing a smooth pathway between the mixing site and the formwork. If the ground is particularly well-compacted and free from bumps you should have few problems; if not, lay a number of stout planks or scaffold boards across the site and drive pegs against the sides at regular intervals to stop them from moving (fig B).

You may need to construct a number of small ramps or bridges along the way: try to support these at least every 2m, either with bricks or trestles (see pages 2066 to 2071). You will need a similar run for a wheelbarrow type mixer if you intend to tip it directly into the formwork. In this case rig up a fairly gradual ramp consisting of two planks, parallel with one another and in line with the mixer

14 Having shovelled in the rest of the aggregate, add more water gradually until the ingredients are well mixed and fall off the drum blades cleanly

15 If you are leaving the mixer in one place, empty the mixed concrete into a wheelbarrow. Be sure to keep the mixer turning as you do so

16 Use scaffold boards and bricks to smooth out any steps or bumps on the route to the site. Make sure the ramps are secure—concrete is heavy

17 Have a heavy timber baulk ready at the site and use it as a step against which to tip the wheelbarrow. Take care not to strain your back

18 With a barrow type mixer, you can often transfer the mixed concrete directly to the site. Again, use a step and keep the drum turning

19 Once you have poured the concrete, a heavy duty vibrator is very useful for settling it and removing airlocks which cause structural faults

Jon Bouchier

wheels. When using such a ramp make absolutely sure that the mixer wheels stay centred on the boards and that the mixer is under complete control at all times—especially when you are tipping.

Before you start mixing, decide on the quantity of concrete you want in each load. If you are a little uncertain, start with small loads and work up to larger ones: full barrows are very heavy and there is no sense in straining yourself or the walkway you have built.

Start off using a bucket as a standard measure; then, as you get more proficient, shovel the ingredients directly into the mixer (see pages 527 to 530). There is no need to hurl materials into the drum: it is far better to let them fall over the lip. Any waste which drops to the ground can be cleared away and re-used.

Start the mixing by putting half the aggregate into the drum. Follow this with half the water and then let the two mix for a few seconds before adding the whole of the cement. Then pour in the rest of aggregate and add more water gradually until you achieve the correct consistency. The mix should fall off the drum blades cleanly, but must not be too wet. If in doubt, turn off the motor and apply the 'squeeze test' (see page 528).

The time you allow the machine to mix will vary according to the amount of material and the exact ratio of cement and aggregate, but on average it should take no longer than three minutes. Once this time has elapsed, you can tip the concrete into a waiting wheelbarrow or directly into the formwork. However, do not switch off: instead keep the motor running then slowly but steadily tip up the machine or turn the control wheel until the whole drum has emptied of its concrete load (fig. 15).

20 *Afterwards, all that remains is to skim the concrete level with the top of the formwork and tamp it down using a timber tamping bar*

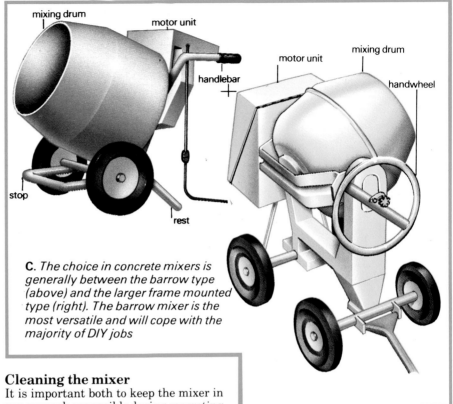

C. *The choice in concrete mixers is generally between the barrow type (above) and the larger frame mounted type (right). The barrow mixer is the most versatile and will cope with the majority of DIY jobs*

Bernard Fallon

Cleaning the mixer
It is important both to keep the mixer in use as much as possible during concreting and to clean it thoroughly after use. If you do not, cement will soon harden on all the surfaces—especially the inside of the drum—and the mixer will become steadily less efficient to the point where it is almost unusable.

As soon as you have tipped one load, fill up the drum with half the aggregate and half the water and leave it running. Even in you do not intend to mix up another load immediately—because you are tamping the concrete, for instance—this will clear the blades ready for action.

At the end of the day clean the mixer thoroughly. Wipe the outside of the machine with a wet rag and leave the motor running for about 15 minutes with a mixture of aggregate and water inside the drum. Then switch off, dump the load and clean off any remaining deposits with a wire brush or the end of a piece of batten. Finally, hose down the entire machine (disconnect an electric mixer first) and leave it to dry off before moving it under cover for the night.

General safety precautions
● Stand to one side when loading the mixer; sometimes a machine will spit material out of the drum mouth.
● Make sure you are standing on a firm footing when loading or tipping the mixer.
● Keep well clear of moving parts. Never reach into the drum with hands or tools while it is rotating.

● Follow the manufacturers' instructions on maintaining motors, gearboxes, drive belts and so on. Lubricate all moving parts regularly and check bolts and mountings before starting work.

Electric motors
If you use a mixer powered by mains electricity you must of course run a power lead from a nearby power socket. In this case check the following:
● Keep the lead out of wet ground and make sure it cannot get damaged in any way. Use waterproof plugs and sockets as well as heavy duty cable. Never unplug intermediate connections unless the machine has first been unplugged at the power source.
● Try to choose a mixer which is double insulated, if possible. An earthed mixer should be fitted with a leakage circuit breaker to prevent accidents.
● Keep water clear of the motor. Never wash down the outside of the machine unless it is unplugged, and wait until it has dried before using it again.
● It is important to be able to switch the motor on and off at the mixer rather than at some remote power socket.
● If you notice a slight voltage drop, it may be that either the cable is kinked or the run between the mains and the machine is too long. If the voltage drop still persists once you have straightened the lead, fit a thicker cable.

A plywood dinghy – 2

Concluding the construction of the plywood dinghy, Part 2 details fitting out the basic hull. Fit seats and duckboards, and you are ready to equip it with rowlocks, motor plates or sails, a mast, centreboard and rudder

Whether your tastes are for rowing, outboard motor power or sailing, your dinghy can be equipped to suit them. Fitting it out for the first two is relatively quick and easy but if you wish it is always possible to add the more expensive and complicated sailing fittings later.

To start with, the hull must be fitted out with duckboards (to protect the bottom) and seats. The duckboards are simply cut from plywood and fitted with strips of hardwood. Just lay them in place in the hull after varnishing. The seats are cut from 12mm plywood and sandwiched between strips of plywood glued to the sides. The centre seat is supported on the centreboard case – the other two have plywood centre supports. Additional inflatable buoyancy bags can be fitted under the rear seat, where they should be secured by lashing. If you are not sailing the dinghy, you will also need a cover for the centreboard case and this can be made from plywood and hardwood scraps.

For rowing, you will need five rowlocks, which can be bought from yacht chandlers. Fix their mounting plates to hardwood blocks and attach these to the gunwales at the points shown.

To prepare for an outboard motor, just fix a plywood mounting plate to the outside of the transom. Similar reinforcing plates are already fixed to the inside of the hull. Most small outboard motors of 4 kilowatts (5hp) or less will be suitable.

To sail the dinghy, you will need a mast and sail. You will also need a centreboard and rudder.

The centreboard and rudder are both made from plywood and hardwood. The rudder is hinged to allow the blade to be lifted for beaching; an elastic cord holds it down at other times. Shape the blade to streamline it as shown. Mortise and tenon the tiller in place. It should be carved to shape to form a comfortable handle. Hang it on rudder pintles (from a yacht chandlers).

Make the mast from aluminium or hardwood. The sail is made from terylene sail cloth panels. Note that these are tapered to give a fullness to the centre. Add reinforcements, eyelets and the boom tube. The boom is in two parts joined at the centre with a sleeve. Tie the sail to the boom and add the rigging.

Finish all timber with yacht varnish, and you are ready to sail. Wear a life jacket at all times in case of accidents.

Ray Duns

Workplan

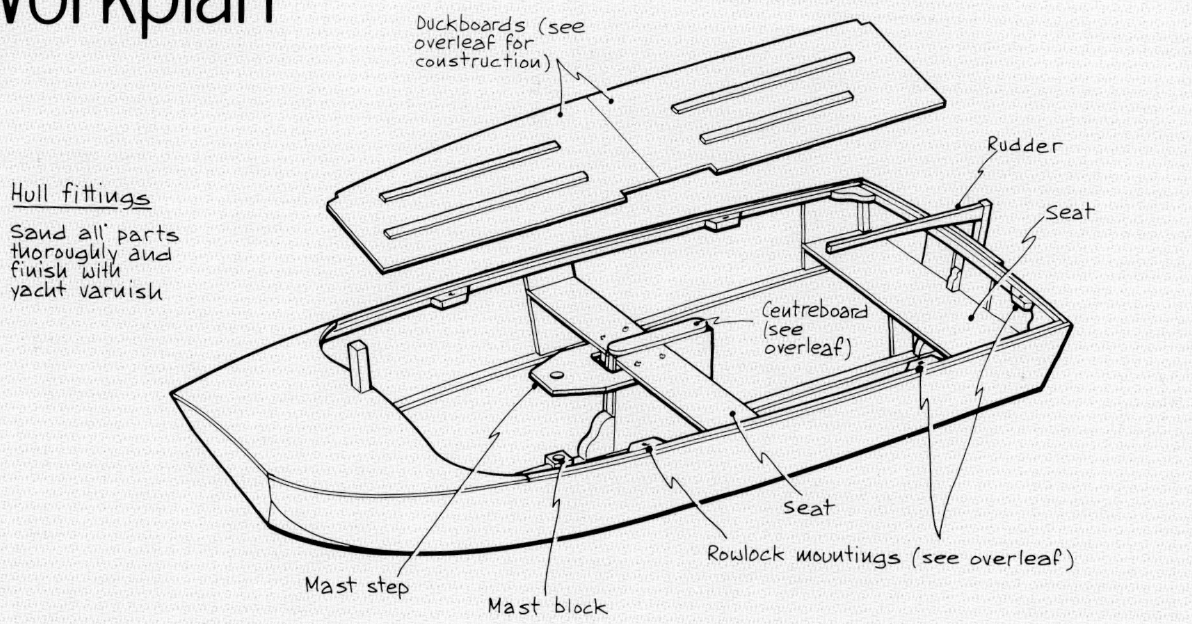

Duckboards (see overleaf for construction)

Rudder

Seat

Hull fittings

Sand all parts thoroughly and finish with yacht varnish

Centreboard (see overleaf)

Seat

Rowlock mountings (see overleaf)

Mast step

Mast block

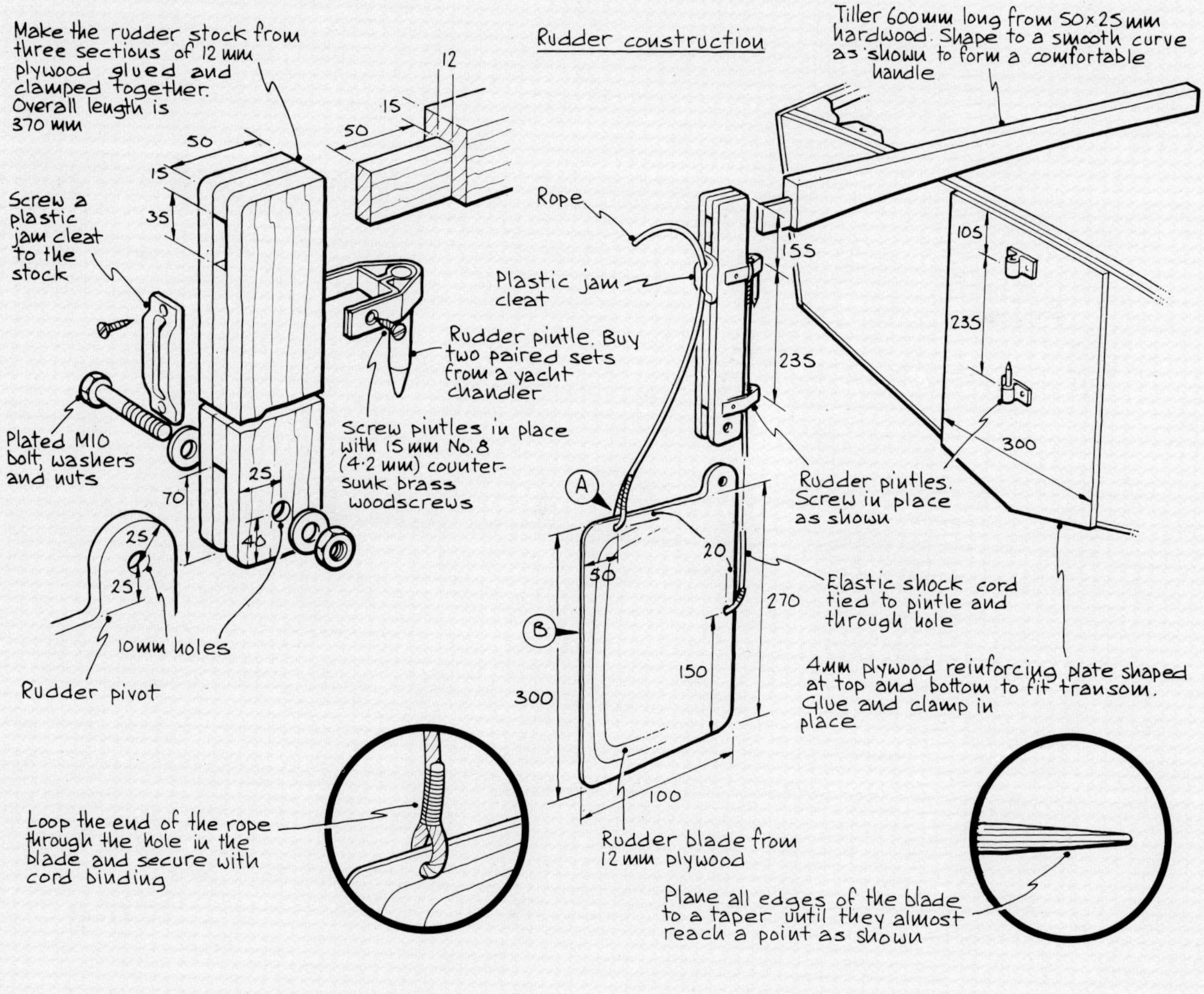

Make the rudder stock from three sections of 12 mm plywood glued and clamped together. Overall length is 370 mm

Rudder construction

Tiller 600 mm long from 50 x 25 mm hardwood. Shape to a smooth curve as shown to form a comfortable handle

Screw a plastic jam cleat to the stock

12

50

15

50

15

35

Rope

Plastic jam cleat

155

105

Rudder pintle. Buy two paired sets from a yacht chandler

235

235

Plated M10 bolt, washers and nuts

Screw pintles in place with 15 mm No. 8 (4·2 mm) countersunk brass woodscrews

70

25

25

40

25

25

10 mm holes

Rudder pivot

A

B

50

20

270

150

300

100

300

Rudder piltes. Screw in place as shown

Elastic shock cord tied to pintle and through hole

4 mm plywood reinforcing plate shaped at top and bottom to fit transom. Glue and clamp in place

Loop the end of the rope through the hole in the blade and secure with cord binding

Rudder blade from 12 mm plywood

Plane all edges of the blade to a taper until they almost reach a point as shown

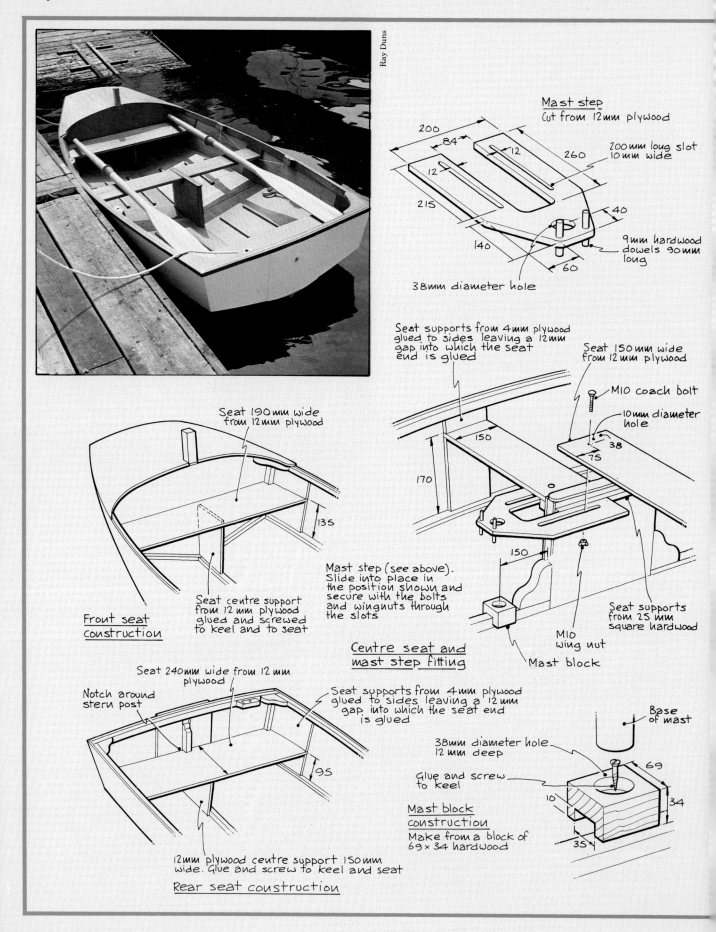

Ray Duns

Mast step
Cut from 12mm plywood

200

84

12

260

200mm long slot
10mm wide

12

215

40

140

9mm hardwood
dowels 90mm
long

60

38mm diameter hole

Seat supports from 4mm plywood
glued to sides leaving a 12mm
gap into which the seat
end is glued

Seat 150mm wide
from 12mm plywood

M10 coach bolt

10mm diameter
hole

150

38

75

170

Seat 190mm wide
from 12mm plywood

135

150

Mast step (see above).
Slide into place in
the position shown and
secure with the bolts
and wingnuts through
the slots

Seat centre support
from 12mm plywood
glued and screwed
to keel and to seat

Seat supports
from 25mm
square hardwood

M10
wing nut

Mast block

**Front seat
construction**

**Centre seat and
mast step fitting**

Seat 240mm wide from 12mm
plywood

Notch around
stern post

Seat supports from 4mm plywood
glued to sides leaving a 12mm
gap into which the seat end
is glued

Base
of mast

38mm diameter hole
12mm deep

Glue and screw
to keel

69

95

10

34

**Mast block
construction**
Make from a block of
69 × 34 hardwood

35

12mm plywood centre support 150mm
wide. Glue and screw to keel and seat

Rear seat construction

Rowlock positions Mount as shown at right

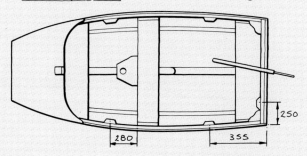

250
280 355

Mounting the rowlocks

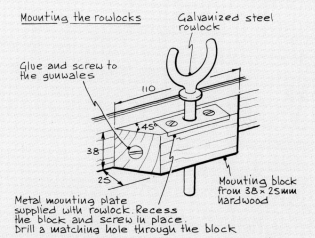

Galvanized steel rowlock

Glue and screw to the gunwales

110
45°
38
25

Metal mounting plate supplied with rowlock. Recess the block and screw in place. Drill a matching hole through the block

Mounting block from 38 × 25mm hardwood

Cutting plan for footboards

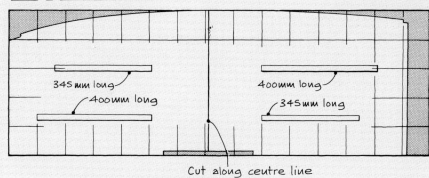

345mm long
400mm long
400mm long
345mm long

Cut along centre line

Each square on the diagram represents 100mm full size. Scale up and transfer to a sheet of 4 mm marine plywood. Glue and screw the hardwood ribs (all from 20 × 12 mm hardwood) in place. Cut two of each board and glue strips to opposite sides

Centreboard (dagger board) construction

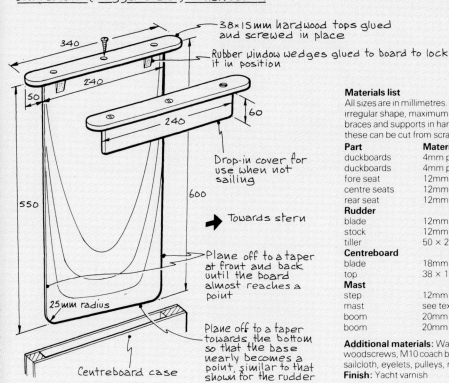

340
240
50
240
60
550
600

38×15mm hardwood tops glued and screwed in place

Rubber window wedges glued to board to lock it in position

Drop-in cover for use when not sailing

→ Towards stern

Plane off to a taper at front and back until the board almost reaches a point

25mm radius

Plane off to a taper towards the bottom so that the base nearly becomes a point, similar to that shown for the rudder

Centreboard case

Materials list

All sizes are in millimetres. All plywood is marine ply (see Part 1). Where parts are of irregular shape, maximum dimensions are given (marked *). Various additional braces and supports in hardwood and plywood are needed. Where unspecified, these can be cut from scrap.

Part	Material	No.	Size
duckboards	4mm plywood	2	720 × 500mm*
duckboards	4mm plywood	2	700 × 500mm*
fore seat	12mm plywood	1	915 × 190mm*
centre seats	12mm plywood	2	535 × 150mm*
rear seat	12mm plywood	1	975 × 240mm*
Rudder			
blade	12mm plywood	1	350 × 100mm*
stock	12mm plywood	3	370 × 50mm*
tiller	50 × 25mm hardboard	1	600mm
Centreboard			
blade	18mm plywood	1	600 × 240mm*
top	38 × 15mm hardwood	1	340mm
Mast			
step	12mm plywood	1	400 × 200mm
mast	see text	1	3000mm
boom	20mm hardwood dowel	1	1950mm
boom	20mm hardwood dowel	1	2250mm

Additional materials: Waterproof woodworking adhesive, brass countersunk woodscrews, M10 coach bolts and wing nuts, screweyes, eyebolts, 170g terylene sailcloth, eyelets, pulleys, rope, pintles, rowlocks
Finish: Yacht varnish

Project

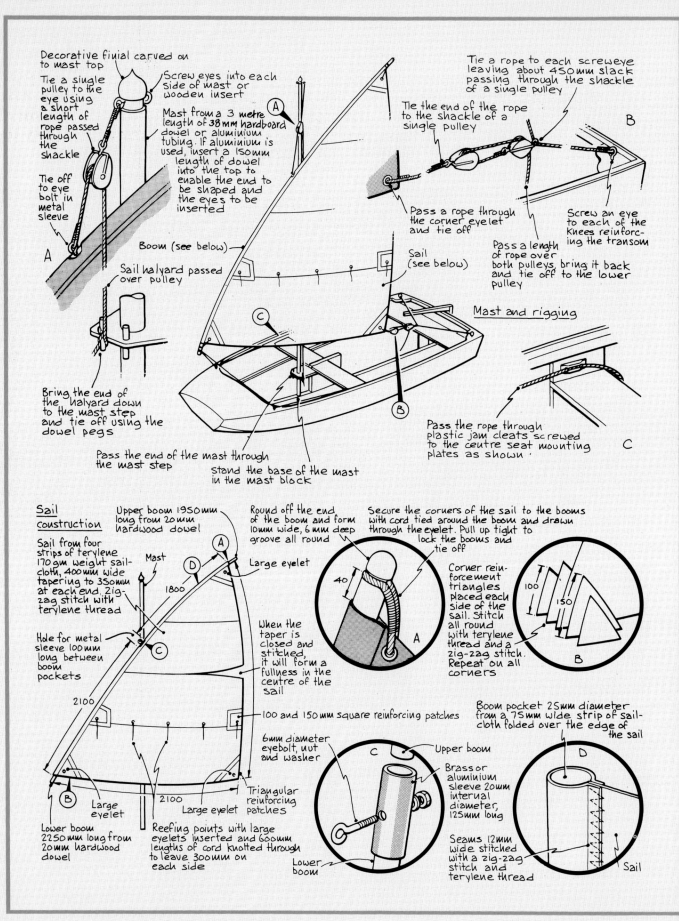

Decorative finial carved on to mast top

Tie a single pulley to the eye using a short length of rope passed through the shackle

Tie off to eye bolt in metal sleeve

A

Screw eyes into each side of mast or wooden insert

Mast from a 3 metre length of 38mm hardboard dowel or aluminium tubing. If aluminium is used, insert a 150mm length of dowel into the top to enable the end to be shaped and the eyes to be inserted

A

Boom (see below)

Sail halyard passed over pulley

Bring the end of the halyard down to the mast step and tie off using the dowel pegs

Pass the end of the mast through the mast step

Stand the base of the mast in the mast block

Tie a rope to each screweye leaving about 450mm slack passing through the shackle of a single pulley

Tie the end of the rope to the shackle of a single pulley

B

Pass a rope through the corner eyelet and tie off

Sail (see below)

Pass a length of rope over both pulleys, bring it back and tie off to the lower pulley

Screw an eye to each of the knees reinforcing the transom

Mast and rigging

C

B

Pass the rope through plastic jam cleats screwed to the centre seat mounting plates as shown

C

Sail construction

Sail from four strips of terylene 170 gm weight sailcloth, 400mm wide tapering to 350mm at each end. Zig-zag stitch with terylene thread

Hole for metal sleeve 100mm long between boom pockets

Upper boom 1950mm long from 20mm hardwood dowel

Mast

A
D
C

1800

2100

B

Large eyelet

2100

Large eyelet

Lower boom 2250mm long from 20mm hardwood dowel

Reefing points with large eyelets inserted and 600mm lengths of cord knotted through to leave 300mm on each side

Round off the end of the boom and form 10mm wide, 6mm deep groove all round

Large eyelet

When the taper is closed and stitched, it will form a fullness in the centre of the sail

100 and 150mm square reinforcing patches

6mm diameter eyebolt, nut and washer

Triangular reinforcing patches

Secure the corners of the sail to the booms with cord tied around the boom and drawn through the eyelet. Pull up tight to lock the booms and tie off

40

A

Corner reinforcement triangles placed each side of the sail. Stitch all round with terylene thread and a zig-zag stitch. Repeat on all corners

100

150

B

Boom pocket 25mm diameter from a 75mm wide strip of sailcloth folded over the edge of the sail

Upper boom

Brass or aluminium sleeve 20mm internal diameter, 125mm long

C

Lower boom

D

Seams 12mm wide stitched with a zig-zag stitch and terylene thread

Sail

Garden storage

Given time, even the smallest garden can land you with a mountain of things to store – be they pot plants and tools or outdoor furniture. A shed usually provides the answer, but there's plenty to think about before making a choice

Whatever size garden you have, you are sure to need some form of storage out of doors for 'garden equipment' – whether for the tools you need to keep the garden from turning into an overgrown and unattractive wilderness, or for furniture and other accoutrements, indispensible if you are to enjoy the garden to the full.

Before deciding on the type of storage facilities to instal, however, it is important to evaluate the extent of your requirements and assess just how much storage space you really need.

Basic considerations

Of course you may already have firm ideas about just how big your garden storage problem is, especially if you have nowhere to store anything. On the other hand, you may be struggling along with thoroughly inadequate facilities, and wondering how to cope.

If your garden tools consist of nothing more than a fork, spade, pair of shears and a small lawn mower, then they could probably all be stored on shelves or hooks on the garage wall. On the other hand, if you have a large garden, with a vegetable plot as well, your garden tool inventory might well encompass two lawn mowers, a cultivator, a number of other power garden tools, plus a full range of hand tools and all the garden chemicals and equipment vital to the keen gardener.

Then there is the question of garden furniture and leisure equipment to consider. Unless you are in the habit of carrying a chair out from the house every time you want to sit in the sun, you will need somewhere to store at least a couple of deckchairs or sunloungers, and perhaps a table as well.

Quite often it makes sense to combine a garden storage zone with space for a workshop or other activities. For example, the vegetable gardener may also need somewhere to store crops – potatoes, apples and so on – after harvesting, and also a potting shed for spring-time planting activities. The home handyman could combine garden storage with a workshop where he can also store tools and materials. And the family may simply want additional leisure space – an outdoor playroom or sun lounge.

The garden shed

If you decide that your needs are for storage only, your choice of facilities is

Right: *A garden shed for a keen grower: the pitched roof with rafters provides plenty of hanging space while shelving and racks take care of everything else*

Jessica Strang

Home designer

fairly straightforward – a traditional garden shed. This can be little bigger than a cupboard, to hold a few garden tools and provide room for a couple of chairs. Or it can be big enough to store mowers and cultivators, wheelbarrows and sacks of potatoes.

In either case, there is a wide choice of styles, shapes and materials from which to choose. The simplest garden shed consists of a wooden rectangle or square, with a floor area of $0.5m^2$ to $1.5m^2$, plus a pent (sloping) roof, a door and no windows – although the roof may be of translucent plastic to let in some light. Larger wooden sheds come with either pent or ridge roofs and probably incorporate at least one window. Those with ridge roofs offer more headroom and provide useful storage space for longer items such as beanpoles.

Alternatively, there are concrete sheds – consisting of prefabricated panels that are bolted together to make up a square or rectangular structure, with windows and doors – and easy-to-erect panelled buildings with a simple framework clad with weatherproof panels. Again, there is a wide range of shapes and sizes available to suit your requirements.

Apart from size and style, there are one or two practical points to bear in mind when choosing a storage shed. Firstly, it must have a lock: many burglaries are committed with the aid of tools taken from unlocked garden sheds; and as well as being extremely expensive, it might prove impossible to replace many of the tools that have been collected over a number of years.

Secondly, it must be totally dry – not just weatherproof – so that tools do not rust and stores do not rot. This means providing a suspended timber floor, rather than a concrete base or a few paving slabs. Ideally, the inner walls of the shed should be lined with some form of insulating board. Such improvements are well worthwhile in the long run, even if they do add to the initial cost and effort of building the shed.

Storage/workroom

If you have decided that you need a workroom as well as a storeroom, then you will want a somewhat larger building. The actual size will, of course, depend on your requirements and the space you have available, but the minimum size you should consider for the purpose is about $1.8 \times 3m$, with good headroom over the entire floor area. So choose a ridge rather than a pent roof.

One end of the building can then be designated for storage (and will therefore

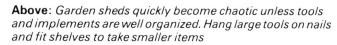

Above: *Garden sheds quickly become chaotic unless tools and implements are well organized. Hang large tools on nails and fit shelves to take smaller items*

Left and above left: *Before and after shots of an ugly storage bunker cleverly disguised with a fast growing creeper – the same can be done to a shed*

Right: *A redundant doorway adapted for garden storage: a window replaces the original door and the bunker below has access from both inside and out*

Michael Warren

Kim Sayer

Jerry Tubby/EWA

not need a window), while the other end can be used as a potting shed or workshop with a window at waist-level to admit adequate light. This arrangement also ensures that you have plenty of wall space for shelves and other storage arrangements.

Comfort will be important if you are going to work for long periods in the shed. A suspended timber floor will again be an asset here, although you may need to consider ways of setting workbench legs on a concrete screed below the floor level to provide a firm work surface for carpentry and similar jobs. Bear in mind too that a concrete shed will be warmer than a timber one in cold weather, unless the latter is lined on the inside.

Storage/summerhouse

You may feel that your additional requirements are not so much for space to work in as for space in which to relax – somewhere to sit in a comfortable chair out of the wind on bright, but chilly days. In this case what you need is a summerhouse, which can also double as an outdoor playroom for the children as well as providing storage space for gardening equipment. Do take care, however, to place any garden chemicals or sharp implements on shelves well out of the reach of children's inquiring hands.

There is a choice of timber outbuildings ranging in style from modern and rustic to the 'Swiss chalet' look. The biggest choice is in cedar or other softwoods and especially useful are those types with casement windows and glazed panelled doors. In fine weather these can all be opened up to admit plenty of fresh air to provide the perfect environment where you can just sit and relax and enjoy the peace and quiet of the garden.

Siting the building

Apart from the obvious practical aspects of size and style, it is important to consider the appearance of the building in the garden – whether you want to make it a feature of the garden or disguise it to blend in with its immediate surroundings.

Although it is mainly a question of personal taste, it is well worth looking at as many different types and styles as possible and considering all the options before committing yourself to spending money on a building that might look totally out of character with your garden once it is erected.

Timber outbuildings, especially cedar ones, look very attractive when new but need regular applications of wood preservative or paint, and also occasional re-roofing with new roofing felt. Concrete buildings, on the other hand, need

virtually no maintenance, and those with a simulated brick and stone finish can look extremely effective.

Sheds that are intended purely for storage are best sited where they are most needed. For example, a storage shed for garden tools and equipment might be most practically positioned at the bottom of the garden, while one used mainly for storing garden furniture could go near the back of the house – to one side of the patio or backing on to the garage.

A combined storage/workshop will obviously be of most use near the house and a storage potting shed near to the flower beds or the vegetable garden. A summer house on the other hand should be positioned according to the geography of the garden to catch the maximum sunlight for the longest part of the day.

It is worth remembering that a building used for any kind of garden storage must be easily accessible, and it might be worth laying a permanent path leading to it which will be passable in wet, as well as in dry, weather.

Give some thought too to whether you will need a supply of electricity to the shed. If it is to be used as a workshop, this will probably be vital for driving power tools and for providing light and warmth. Remember that an outbuilding should be supplied via a permanent and separate

Michael Nicholson/EWA

electrical circuit taken from the house's main fuseboard, and that the cables should either be buried in the ground or carried overhead to the building out of harm's way (see pages 1965 to 1970).

If you do not want to make a feature of your garden shed, it can be tucked away to one side or placed at the bottom of the garden, and screened from the house with quick-growing conifers, fencing or a screen block wall. Alternatively, it can be stained or painted to blend in with its surroundings, or covered with climbing plants such as ivy.

Storage alternatives

If you feel that a separate outbuilding is not the solution to your garden storage problems, there are one or two other ideas you could consider.

The first is to build a simple lean-to structure against the back wall of the house to provide lockable storage space for a few garden tools or a small selection of fold-away garden furniture. Such a structure need be only about 600mm deep with a sloping roof and a hinged door. The inside walls can be lined with polyethylene, stapled to the woodwork to help keep the damp out, and the junction between the new structure and the house sealed to prevent water penetration.

Another idea is to construct a small porch or conservatory outside the back door of the house—again a lean-to building, but this time mainly glazed to admit optimum light—to provide not only the necessary storage space, but also somewhere to raise houseplants, keep muddy shoes and even dry the washing on wet days. This type of structure would have the added bonus of cutting down on draughts inside the house and heat loss through the back door.

Below: *Hoses often cause more clutter than anything else. The answer is a capstan with its own water supply*

Michael Nicholson/EWA

A vegetable rack

Ray Duns

Build this simple low-cost rack to help you make the best use of the space available in your garden shed. Use it either for garden produce or for storing bulbs over the winter.

It is based on a timber frame which forms trays on five levels. The tray bases are made from wire mesh. Although the timber sizes specified are ideal, you can use any available offcuts if they are of approximately the same dimensions. You could, for example, use thicker timber for the tray sides. Note however that the tray front rails are designed to be lower than the sides or the backs, so that you can reach in easily.

Cut out all the timber parts to the appropriate lengths. Finish is not critical, so it does not matter if you are using slightly sub-standard wood, but you should remove any splinters. Assemble with glue and nails, checking the alignment with a square. Start by making up the front and back, joining the uprights with the cross rails, then join these two together with the side rails.

When the assembly is complete turn it upside down and fix the bases in place, working from the lowest one up. Make the bases from chicken wire mesh (the plastic coated variety resists corrosion better) held to the frame with small netting staples. Cut the mesh oversize and pull it tight. Trim after fixing and bend any sharp ends under to ensure that they will not damage the fruit or bulbs.

There is no need to seal or paint any of the timber, although you can if you prefer so long as you choose a non-toxic variety.

Use the rack for storing vegetable crops before they are brought into the house, or for keeping them through the winter. You should only do this, however, if your shed is frost proof. Crops such as apples, which should be kept separate, can be stored in divided apple trays which are often discarded by greengrocers or market traders.

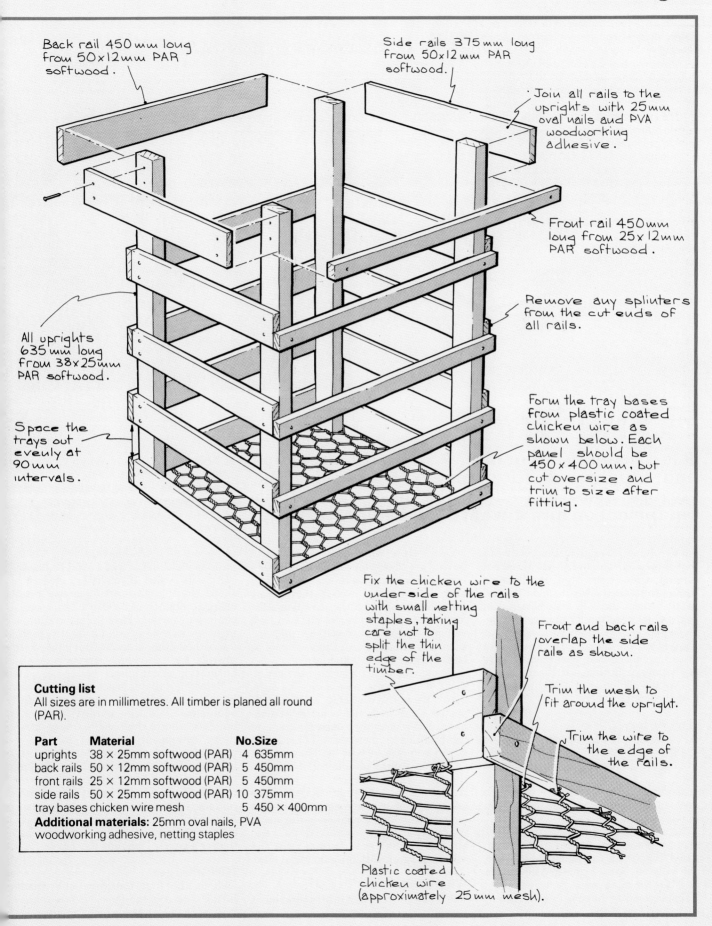

Back rail 450 mm long from 50×12 mm PAR softwood.

Side rails 375 mm long from 50×12 mm PAR softwood.

Join all rails to the uprights with 25 mm oval nails and PVA woodworking adhesive.

Front rail 450 mm long from 25×12 mm PAR softwood.

Remove any splinters from the cut ends of all rails.

All uprights 635 mm long from 38×25 mm PAR softwood.

Space the trays out evenly at 90 mm intervals.

Form the tray bases from plastic coated chicken wire as shown below. Each panel should be 450×400 mm, but cut oversize and trim to size after fitting.

Fix the chicken wire to the underside of the rails with small netting staples, taking care not to split the thin edge of the timber.

Front and back rails overlap the side rails as shown.

Trim the mesh to fit around the upright.

Trim the wire to the edge of the rails.

Plastic coated chicken wire (approximately 25 mm mesh).

Cutting list

All sizes are in millimetres. All timber is planed all round (PAR).

Part	Material	No.	Size
uprights	38 × 25mm softwood (PAR)	4	635mm
back rails	50 × 12mm softwood (PAR)	5	450mm
front rails	25 × 12mm softwood (PAR)	5	450mm
side rails	50 × 25mm softwood (PAR)	10	375mm
tray bases	chicken wire mesh	5	450 × 400mm

Additional materials: 25mm oval nails, PVA woodworking adhesive, netting staples

Home hiring

● **Is it better to buy or hire?** ● **Specialist hire shops and suppliers** ● **Hire charges** ● **Choosing the correct tools** ● **Getting the best value from equipment on hire** ● **What is available**

A. Above: *Hire shops supply a whole range of equipment suitable for domestic use – from simple power tools such as saws and drills to complex scaffolding parts and large excavating and hole-making machinery*

All too often a job crops up that requires a tool or piece of equipment that you do not already own. Usually it is a simple matter to go out and buy it – and if the tool is fairly cheap and will come in useful on other occasions, this is the best option. However, you will sometimes find that the tool you need is either very expensive or so specialized that you are unlikely to need it again. In this case, the solution is to hire the equipment you require from a tool or plant hire shop.

Hire or buy?
At first sight it may appear to be a lot cheaper and more convenient to hire almost all the tools and equipment you need. But in many cases this is false economy and you could save both time and money by buying the equipment outright in the first place.

General tools – such as electric drills – should always be bought rather than hired. Even if the initial outlay is higher, the tools can be used time and time again and it is far more useful to have them at hand instead of having to pay regular visits to a hire shop.

Other tools which it may be worth buying are those you will be using over a long period of time. In this case the cost of hire will greatly exceed the buying price – particularly if the job takes a lot longer than you had at first planned. So if you are tackling a long term project – such as building an extension – it may be better to buy rather than hire.

Remember that if you buy any equipment it need not necessarily be new; many perfectly workable tools can be picked up at reasonable prices secondhand. Keep your eyes open for these in local builders' merchants or look for advertisements in your local newspaper. Of course, it may also be possible to sell the tools and equipment afterwards to recoup some of your outlay. One advantage of this arrangement is that depreciation of secondhand materials is relatively small so you could quite easily buy tools at half their normal price and sell them again with little financial loss.

Where to hire
The most obvious place to hire equipment is from a specialist tool hire shop if there

is one nearby. The shop may be part of a nationwide chain or just a local business run by its owner. If you have a choice of shops check their stock lists and hire charges carefully. A shop in a nationwide chain will usually have far more equipment (or be able to order it for you from one of their other branches) but it may not provide the individual service a small business is able to offer.

Remember that it is not only specialist hire shops which can supply you with equipment. Many garden centres, builders' merchants and garages also hire equipment related to their particular field. Examine their stock list carefully and you may be able to find a greater range of equipment for the job you intend to tackle – often at far more competitive prices. For very large jobs, requiring small trucks and large machinery, you could try a plant hire firm or a general building contractor.

Hire charges
One of the first considerations when hiring tools and equipment is how much it is going to cost. Many hire firms have a

particularly complex set of charges so make sure you understand these before signing any hire agreement.

Many tools are hired at an hourly, daily, weekly or even monthly rate, so it is worth calculating carefully which charge band will work out cheapest for you. When calculating and comparing hire charges, find out for what period you are likely to be charged. Ask whether you will be charged for two whole days if the shop is closed over part of the weekend for instance and whether you can save money by returning tools before the hire period expires.

The hire shop will always want you to leave a deposit on each piece of equipment hired. This is to ensure that the equipment is returned intact; you will lose part of the money if the machine is damaged or has been misused in any way. The amount of deposit required will vary according to the value of the equipment hired but most shops will be willing to accept a cheque or credit card to cover this, which can be returned to you later.

Hire charges come into effect as soon as you leave the shop so it makes sense to keep costs to a minimum. One way of doing this is to plan the work so you can use the equipment for the shortest possible time and return it quickly afterwards.

If you are sanding a timber floor, for instance, do not hire a rotary floor sander until the whole room has been cleared, defects in the boards have been fixed and all protruding nails punched well below the surface. Only then should you collect the sander and start work. When the job has been completed, return the sander to the hire shop soon afterwards.

Choosing tools

When you buy a tool there is normally a wide choice of different brands to choose from so you can usually pick the one that suits you best. But when hiring, you are unlikely to be offered such a choice and may not always get the tool that gives the best performance or is the easiest to use.

This may not matter too much for a short hiring since you can usually put up with a slightly sub-standard tool for a while. But if you hire a piece of equipment which turns out to be completely unsuitable or even potentially dangerous, you have a right to complain. Take it back to the shop and explain what is wrong. They may replace it or at very least explain how the tool can be used more effectively and safely.

You can avoid these sorts of problems in the first place by checking the equipment thoroughly before you leave the shop. Ask the owner or assistant for advice in choosing the correct tool and make sure that you know how to use it.

Never be tempted to hire a tool just because it is the largest and most powerful in the range. Apart from being more costly, such a tool will be heavier and more difficult to control and should only be used where absolutely necessary.

Tools and equipment for hire

Although you can hire practically anything if you search hard enough the list below gives a fair indication of the tools and equipment which are available.

Ladders and scaffolding

Ladders: Both wooden and aluminium ladders can be hired. For large jobs aluminium ladders are lighter and easier

B. Below: *Heavy-duty cleaners can be hired to renovate carpets and other floor coverings.* **Above right**: *Load the machine with solvent and hot water.* **Left**: *Spray the carpet and vacuum off any excess water.* **Below right**: *Empty the dirty waste into a bucket*

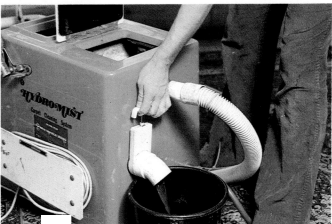

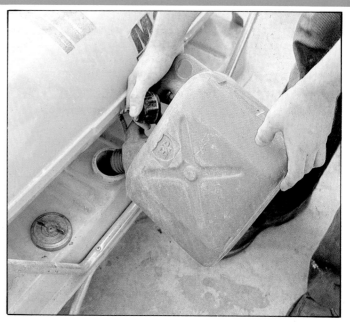

C. Left: *A space heater is an ideal means of warming up any enclosed area—such as a workshop or outhouse—where the temperature is often too cold to work comfortably.*
Above: *The heater is powered by an electrically driven fan and burns paraffin (kerosene)*

D. Below left to right: *Using a wallpaper stripper. First fill the machine with water and switch on. Once the plate starts to steam—usually after only a few minutes—press it to the wall and hold it there for a few seconds. The loosened paper can then be stripped off*

to use. Choose a ladder that is slightly longer than you actually need so it is safe to use (see pages 532 to 536).

When hiring ladders ask about accessories which will make work safer—such as ladder stays and tool trays.
Scaffolding: For large-scale projects which require you to work at heights for a considerable period of time, scaffolding is essential. For simple jobs up to first floor level you can use decorator's trestles and simple staging (see pages 401 to 405). For higher or more complex jobs you can use either a simple scaffolding tower (see pages 532 to 536) or erect independent or tied scaffolding (see pages 772 to 777).

You will be charged at a rate per metre of scaffolding tube hired so work out what you need before ordering. Some hire shops will erect and dismantle the scaffolding for you.

Decorating tools
There is little scope for hiring simple decorating tools since most are inexpensive to buy. However, some larger items are fairly popular.
Floor sanders: If you want to sand your floor prior to lacquering the whole surface you will need a large floor sander as well as a belt or orbital sander to reach into the corners (see pages 860 to 863).

Sanding sheets are usually available on sale or return, so always take more than you need so there is no danger of running out while the shop is closed.
Wallpaper strippers: There are machines for rapid removal of wallpaper and lining paper prior to redecoration. To aid stripping most machines are fed by a paraffin (kerosene) or an electrically operated steam unit. Steam is forced through a feed pipe into the base of a broad flat plate which is used to soften the paper prior to stripping.

Before you use the machine clear the room of furniture and cover the floor either with sheets of polyethelene or

George Wright

newspaper. This will protect the furnishings and make it easier to clear up scraps of wallpaper afterwards.

Fill the steam unit with water, switch it on and wait until it heats up. When working with the stripper start from the bottom of the wall and work upwards. Force the plate hard against the wall, and hold it there for a few seconds. Some of the more stubborn patches may have to be covered a number of times before they are completely removed.

Paint sprayers: Spray painting can be four or five times faster than by brush or roller (see pages 1264 to 1267 and 1308 to 1312). You can hire an electrically operated airless sprayer, or for larger jobs an electric or petrol-driven compressor unit. The spray will come complete with a number of different nozzles which are necessary so that you can tackle a variety of different materials.

Building tools

This is an area where the range of tools for hire is enormous. At the top end of the range are large excavating and hole digging machines which are usually available only from large plant hire firms, but smaller pieces of equipment – such as mixers and concrete breakers –

are available from smaller hire shops. Concreting tools are dealt with in detail on pages 2386 to 2391.

Electric drills: You probably already own a standard two or three-speed electric drill but this cannot always cope with heavy-duty work and the size of bit it can handle is often limited. Most hire shops have a variety of industrial drills capable of making large diameter holes in almost any type of material (see pages 1606 to 1611).

Hand tools: If you decide to tackle a large building project with the help of friends you may not always have enough of the basic tools to go around. Most hire shops will be able to help you out by supplying items such as shovels, picks, wheelbarrows and so on.

Welding: Small mains-powered welding units are available for hire from some shops to help you tackle special repair jobs (see pages 2413 to 2419).

Plumbing tools

Hire shops can supply you with a large number of plumbing tools including **basin spanners** for loosening nuts in restricted areas; **tap reseaters** for curing leaking taps and **slip joint pliers** for connecting and disconnecting immersion

E. Above: *A pipe bending machine is useful if you want to tackle a large-scale plumbing job – such as installing a central heating system. The machine comes complete with a set of formers designed to fit standard pipe sizes*

heaters. But examine the cost of hiring such tools carefully; the hire fee may be only a little less than the price of buying them outright.

Pipe cutting and bending machines are well worth hiring if you do not already own them.

Cutting machines

Chain saws: These are ideal for trimming large branches and cutting through large baulks of timber (see page 1930).

Circular saws: For cutting planks and boards quickly and exactly a circular saw is an indispensable tool. You may even want to hire a saw bench which allows even greater accuracy and speed (see pages 1925 to 1930).

Angle grinders: These can be used for grinding metal and sharpening axes and lawn mower blades, but they are more commonly used for cutting both metal and masonry (see page 1930).

Building a greenhouse

● **The advantages of building a greenhouse from scratch** ● **Basic considerations to bear in mind** ● **Design and construction of basic lean-to assemblies—one clad with PVC corrugated roofing sheets, and one glazed**

In temperate climates, the growing season for many plants in the open is short, and this is bound to restrict your choice of plants and flowers. But a greenhouse can alter the situation completely, enabling plants of many kinds to be grown all the year round. In colder climates, an even greater variety of plants can be propagated and grown if the greenhouse is heated, as this will allow you to grow exotic examples from warmer regions around the world.

A. Above: *A lean-to greenhouse is a pot planter's paradise and an asset to any home. In it you can be 'outside' and relax even when the weather is bad—and it is far cheaper than an extension*

Building your own greenhouse is not a very complicated job, and it permits you to design and tailor the building to suit your individual needs, the requirements of the site, and the plants that you wish to grow. It can also be surprisingly cheap.

Basic considerations

One of the first things to decide is the type of crop to be grown, noting any special requirements; for example, indoor carnations grow best in tall greenhouses, and need more ventilation than most crops. If you are uncertain about the most suitable greenhouse for your needs consult a nursery or an experienced gardener. However, for average purposes, it is usually a matter of selecting a convenient and sunny spot, either making use of an existing wall to build a lean-to greenhouse, or alternatively siting it apart from other buildings as a free-standing unit.

The size and type of greenhouse best suited to your needs are partly governed by the space available, the site itself, the crops and the final cost.

The lean-to type, best sited on an east-west axis in the sun, is usually cheaper to make, to heat (because of its better insulation), and to maintain than a free-standing model of similar size and construction. The mini greenhouse variation can be either a lean-to or free-standing type (see below).

Available space may be further restricted by planning regulations. Structures in front of the building line between the house and the road are normally prohibited in the UK. On the other hand small greenhouses which are less than 3m high and which do not occupy more than half the garden area are not usually subject to planning consent. Unless you are absolutely certain of the planning regulations in your area, you should consult the local council before starting work.

Design and construction

All buildings have a number of important design and construction requirements, and in the case of a greenhouse there are six main considerations.

● **Appearance:** This is influenced by the design and also by the construction materials—usually wood and glass.

● **Strength and durability:** A greenhouse should be capable of withstanding the worst possible conditions of wind, sun, storms, frost and snow. Timber glazing bars, for example, should ideally not be less than 20mm deep for a 1m span, and the depth should be increased by 12mm for each additional 500mm of span.

● **Light:** Maximum light is of course necessary all the year round so avoid narrowly spaced glazing bars, aiming for intervals of between 450mm and 750mm.

● **Ventilation:** This is critical, and trials have shown that the total ventilator area should ideally not be less than 15 percent or one-sixth of the floor space.

● **Ease of construction:** It is very important that a greenhouse project does not demand great expense on tools and materials, and in this respect a timber frame is a good choice.

● **Low maintenance:** Costs need to be kept in mind, and simplicity of design, combined with sound construction techniques are of great importance.

Comparison with kits

When deciding whether to erect a proprietary kit greenhouse, or to build a home made unit, the acid test for most people boils down to cost; but to make a valid comparison you have to take into account many factors, including quality, design, construction and durability. Often the kit price excludes such items as the base, the glass and delivery, so the comparison must be made on the cost of the different greenhouses erected on site complete. This way you can make a fair assessment of relative costs.

The materials for a typical built-from-scratch greenhouse are no more than half of the price of a similar kit. And, given that you can take satisfaction from your own labour, making a greenhouse is still an economically worthwhile proposition.

Nature and scope of the models

Although this article describes how to build two lean-to types of greenhouse, a free-standing span or apex type with a high central ridge or a mini greenhouse can also be made with certain modifications.

Timber is excellent for the main structure because it is versatile and easy to work with, and presents few problems with either glazing or cladding. Also, less condensation forms on wooden frames than on metal ones because they retain a more even temperature. Given the occasional treatment with paint or preservative, timber structures can last 20 to 30 years and more.

Softwood should be treated with a horticultural grade of preservative containing copper napthanate (in the UK, a suitable choice would be Cuprinol). Special attention should be paid to joints and those parts of the building which are in contact with the ground. These should be soaked for a few hours in a container of the solution. Long timbers such as bottom plates can be laid on a long sheet of polyethylene gathered along the corners and edges to form a receptacle or bag into which preservative is poured.

Although it costs about 50 percent more, cedar wood is a timber which

requires little treatment or maintenance because it has a natural oil which resists decay and is ideal for outdoor use.

Both the lean-to greenhouse designs are made up of four sections—two ends, the front and the roof. The designs as shown are adequate for a greenhouse with an eaves height of 1.52m, a ridge height of 2.13m and a width of 2.33m. This should allow considerable freedom of movement, but the measurements can easily be adapted to your own requirements, especially the length. However, if and when altering sizes, keep in mind the standard sizes of cladding materials: this avoids needless cutting and subsequent waste. Also, when building larger structures, heavier timbers and bracing are necessary for extra strength.

The four frames of the greenhouse can be assembled in one or two ways. The

frames can be made up separately, then bolted together and screwed to the wall. Alternatively, the wall timbers or studs can be screwed to the wall first, and the framework then constructed in situ. The frame can later be glazed or clad with PVC corrugated roofing sheet (such as Novolux in the UK). Standard 4mm thick glass is adequate for glazing and this should be installed in 'modules' as nearly square as possible. This means in effect that the glass is panelled. For instance, on the roof, each run of glass between timbers consists of three panes of overlapping glass. This avoids the use of large panes of glass which are both vulnerable and difficult to instal.

When planning the greenhouse, remember to allow extra for the width of glass or PVC sheeting 'lost' in channelling grooves or housings.

1 First prepare the site, providing an even bed of hardcore which should be well tamped down, and paint the back wall with a weatherproof agent

2 Having cut the back horizontal and vertical timbers and applied a timber preservative, fix the horizontal wall plate with long coach bolts

3 Once the loadbearing wall plate has been fixed the vertical back frame can be secured to the wall using masonry nails

4 Lay a single course of lightweight building blocks then mortar treated posts into the hollow corner blocks. Make sure that the posts are vertical

John Ward

John Ward

5 *In order to save much wasteful trimming of the cladding material, it makes sense to use it as a guide when actually building the structure*

6 *The bottom plate of the front frame is a structural component and so it should be firmly fixed to the building blocks with wall anchors*

7 *At this stage apply a liberal amount of timber preservative to the bottom plate, making quite certain that you treat all cuts and end grain*

Making the four frames is very simple. The essence of the separate parts is that they are self-bracing, in other words they have an intrinsic strength in their unassembled state. The following is only a guide however, and you should feel free to modify the construction if you want to change the dimensions.

End frame: Using planed softwood timber, cut the base, top, back and front to size then make half-lap angle joints at the ends using a tenon saw and chisel. Make T-halving joints to take the upright and horizontal timbers; these in turn are then cut to size with half-lap joints at the ends. The joints in the top rail must of course be cut to the appropriate angle.

In all cases, paint the prepared cuts with preservative before putting them together. Drill and countersink two screw holes at each joint to take the appropriate screws. Do, however, avoid drilling too deep or the screws will have an insufficient grip. Finally assemble the timber sections and screw them together, making sure that the bottom corners are perfectly square.

End frame with door: Preparation and assembly of the parts is the same as for the first end frame, but with three differences. The lower horizontal timber cross rail from the front stops at the centre upright instead of running through to the back. This allows for the door. Also necessary is a projecting vertical door stop fixed behind the centre upright and aligned with the door.

The door itself is made from two uprights, fixed to three cross pieces with half-lap joints at the ends and T-halving joints in the centre. Drill and countersink the appropriate screws as before. Then fix three 150mm 'T' hinges to the cross members of the door. The door should not actually be hung until the end frames are

8 *Once the preservative is dry, set the bottom plate on the building blocks. Make sure that it is flat then render the building block course*

9 *The PVC roofing sheets can be secured to the structure either with battens or in grooves–the latter being easy to make with a circular saw*

fastened to the wall, but check that the door fits the frame before erecting the structure and adjust as necessary.

Front frame: Cut the four upright timbers to the correct length, making T-halving joints in the centres. Then cut the top, centre and base members, with half-lap end joints, plus two evenly spaced T-halving joints on each. Paint all joints with preservative and allow this to dry before drilling and countersinking to take two screws at each joint. Finally, assemble and screw the timbers together, making sure that the corners are square and that the bottom plate is laid flat side down like those of the end frames. If you decide to put a door in the front frame, follow the instructions given above. As before, do not hang the door until the structure is complete, but do make sure that it fits the frame before moving on to assemble the greenhouse.

11 *Where thin section timbers are butt or halving jointed it is best to secure them with a screw. Always drill holes to avoid splitting the wood*

Roof: Repeat as for the front frame, with the addition of a ventilator seating. Cut the ventilator seating timber with half-lap joints at each end and screw this securely into the extended half-lap joints of the two centre timbers. Because of the sloping roof it is necessary to chamfer the back timber by about 7°, just sufficiently to allow it to butt squarely against the wall when fixed to the wall plate. Make the ventilator frame in the same way as the door, with the necessary size adjustments. Fix two 150mm strap hinges to the roof frame for the ventilator and make sure that it is a good weatherproof fit.

Foundations
The base of the greenhouse must be raised above the ground level, to keep it clear of surface water.

10 *The essence of the greenhouse structure is that the frame is self-bracing. The front top plate is thus nailed to the front corner posts*

12 *Housing joints are normally skew-nailed, but a galvanized steel angle bracket screwed under the joint provides added strength*

If you are building on soil then you will have to dig a foundation to provide a base, the top of which should be at least 25mm above ground level.

It may be that there will be an existing foundation of sorts, in the form of a driveway, path or patio. Providing this consists of paving slabs or concrete laid over a hardcore base it will be adequate, although the level will still have to be raised to the proper height.

One way of doing this is to fit a form-work of 25mm × 25mm battening around the base and fill it with concrete. If you use this method, you must ensure that the new concrete bonds well to the existing surface by coating the latter with a solution of PVA bonding agent.

An alternative is to 'build' the base by laying paving slabs or a layer of bricks – with mortared joints in between them – on the top of the existing surface.

Whichever method you choose, the finished surface must be painted with a proprietary waterproof sealing compound (such as Aquaseal 40 Heavy Duty) to damp-proof it.

The base must be absolutely level when finished otherwise the wooden frames of the greenhouse will be at staggered heights when you come to assemble them and therefore they will not fit.

A far simpler method of isolating the timber frame from the ground is to build a single course of lightweight building blocks on top of a shallow 150mm concrete foundation, then lay the bottom plates on the frames. Using this method, the two front corner posts, suitably preserved, may be anchored into hollow blocks, and the rest of the structure constructed about these (fig. 4). If the course is continued around the floor area, there will be a step at the base of the door.

13 *Alternatively, screw through joints after drilling and plugging the end grain of the longitudinal timber to avoid splitting it with the screw*

If you feel that this is a disadvantage, the blocks and bottom plate can be constructed with a cutout for the door. However, without the step it will be very difficult to both keep the door away from the rot-inducing soil, and to make the greenhouse draughtproof.

The receiving wall
The wall to which the greenhouse is attached should, ideally, be absolutely vertical. Unfortunately few walls are. If the wall is less than 12mm out of plumb, the gap can be filled with a bricklaying mortar. But, if it is over 12mm or you do not want a wedge-shaped mortar gap, then you will have to shape three lengths of 50mm × 50mm timber (two vertical battens support the two end frames, and the horizontal batten – the wall plate – supports the roof) so that they form a vertical surface to which the greenhouse frame will be attached. Use the scribing technique described on page 830, then, having laid a thick layer of sealing mastic or compound along the wall and the timber where the surfaces will meet, screw the timber firmly to the wall with wall plugs or large bolts.

Construction
All the joints should be both glued and screwed, using a waterproof adhesive such as urea formaldehyde and either brass, galvanized or japanned screws. The glass or PVC sheeting can be housed either between narrow wooden battens or in glazing grooves cut with a plough plane, router or power saw.

Assembly
Drill the back plate of one end frame and fix it to the vertical timber attached to the wall, then do the same at the other end frame. Move the front frame into place, drilling and fixing the base to the bolts (which are set in concrete). Drill and screw the ends of the front frame to the respective front timbers of the end frames. The shell of the greenhouse is then ready to receive the roof frame. This should be drilled and fixed to the end and front frames as well as to the wall plate, and when fitting it, you should make quite sure that the frame is flush with the wall to avoid distortion.

PVC
To clad the frame first lay one sheet of PVC roofing on the ventilator (if fitted), bedding it down on foam eaves filler and fixing it with nails and washers. Then fix the casement stay and hinges. Carefully position and secure the remainder of the PVC sheets to the roof, using eaves filler, and securing them with screws and washers (see pages 1526 to 1531).

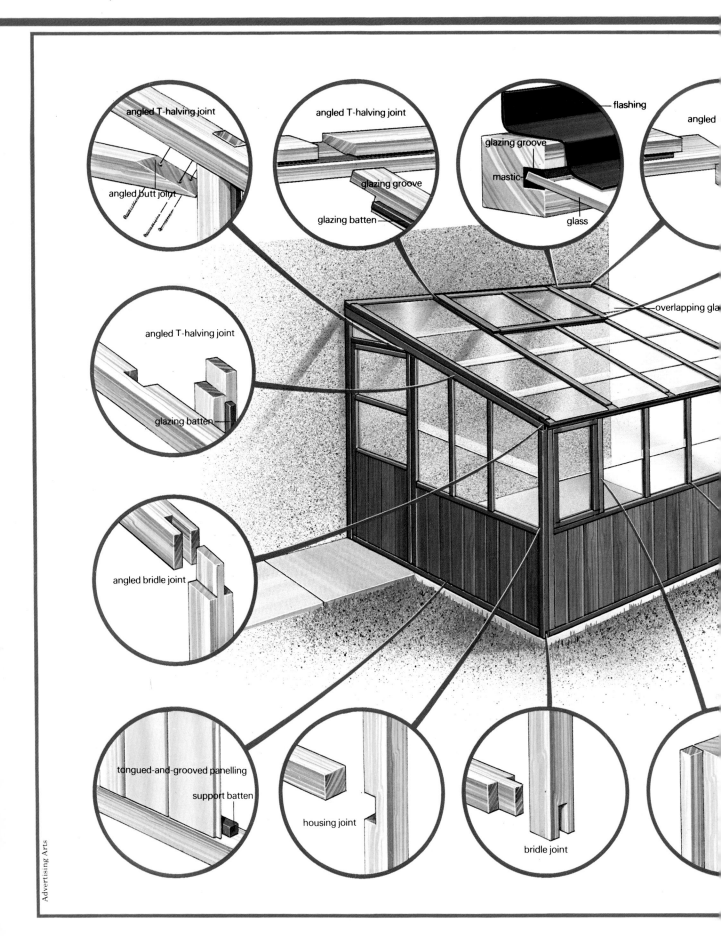

angled T-halving joint

angled butt joint

angled T-halving joint

glazing groove

glazing batten

flashing

glazing groove

mastic

glass

angled

angled T-halving joint

glazing batten

overlapping gla

angled bridle joint

tongued-and-grooved panelling

support batten

housing joint

bridle joint

Advertising Arts

Alternative constructions

The glazed and boarded greenhouse **(left)** has been designed as simply as possible so that it can be constructed with a minimum of time and effort. The generous eaves height of 1520mm and a ridge height of 2130mm ensures adequate headroom, especially around the edges at bench or staging level where plants are sited. And the width of 2330mm allows considerable freedom of movement.

The timber section for the standard sized greenhouse should be at least 50mm × 50mm for all structural components and 75mm × 50mm for the door posts. The door battens should be 25mm × 25mm and the glazing beading should be 16mm × 16mm.

The measurements can be adapted according to your requirements, especially the length. If the design is extended in this way some extra reinforcing will be necessary mid-way along the roof and side. A glazing bar can be replaced by a 75mm × 50mm timber and a cross bar at the side would add rigidity and strength. A similar stout piece of timber should be inserted mid-way along the side section.

Throughout the design two main glass widths—460mm and 610mm—are used. The window and roof glass, it must be noted, is installed in 'modules' as nearly square as possible. This means in effect that the glass is panelled. For instance, on the roof each run of glass between timbers consists of three panes of overlapping glass.

In the case of a PVC sheet clad greenhouse (below) the timber section should be at least 50mm × 50mm. The hardwood corner posts should be 75mm × 75mm, but you can get away with 50mm × 25mm for the wall plate and vertical wall timbers.

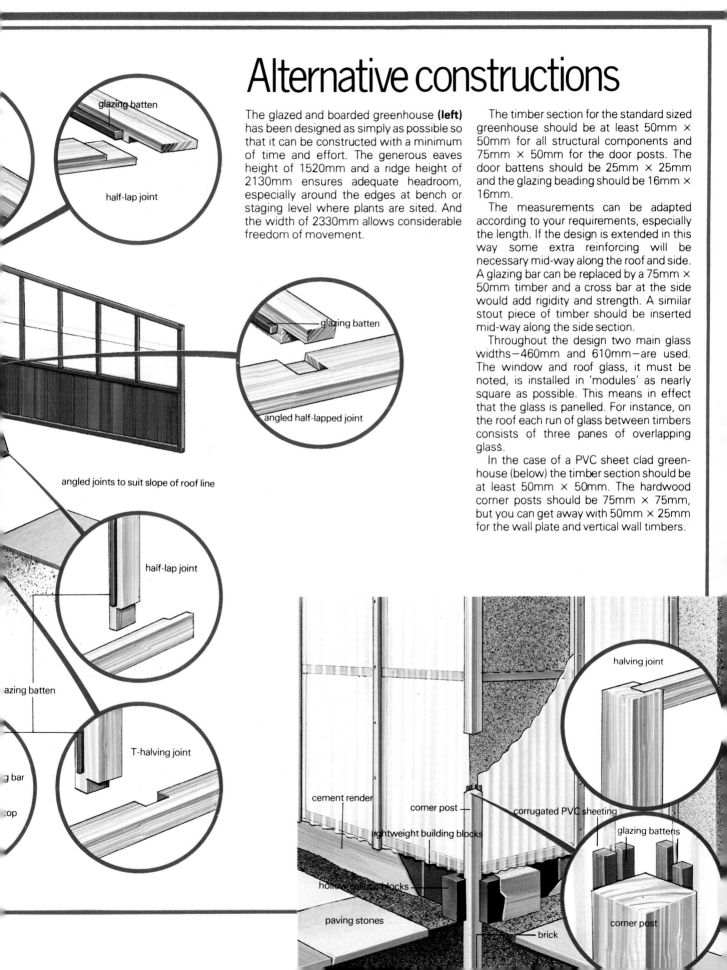

glazing batten

half-lap joint

glazing batten

angled half-lapped joint

angled joints to suit slope of roof line

half-lap joint

azing batten

g bar

op

T-halving joint

halving joint

cement render

corner post

corrugated PVC sheeting

lightweight building blocks

glazing battens

hollow cellular blocks

paving stones

corner post

brick

14 *The PVC sheet can be cut using an abrasive disc fitted to a circular saw or saw attachment. Use a stout length of timber as a fence*

15 *When fixing the PVC cladding, support the sheets from below and from behind then drill through them and into the supporting timber*

16 *Use pre-formed polystyrene eaves filler strips when fitting the roof to provide rigidity and also to draughtproof the greenhouse*

Fix PVC sheeting to the door frame in the same way as to the ventilator, then fix the door in place, making sure that it opens and closes freely. When covering the ends, it is necessary to measure carefully then cut the PVC sheet to shape using a fine toothed saw.

Glazing

The method of overlapping glass panes is quite simple. First press a bed of putty along the glazing beading shelf, then press the bottom pane of glass into the putty. Now hold the next higher pane where it will be fixed, and mark the sides of the structure where the bottom of the pane will be located.

Put the pane aside for the time being and drive a 25mm nail into each side of the woodwork immediately next to the lower pane, level with the marks, until just about 6mm of the head is still protruding. You now have two metal stops on which the next pane can rest while it is puttied in position. The process is repeated for successive panes. There are several types of proprietary clips that are made for joining overlapping glass sheets, but they all suffer from the same disadvantage – the final pane often has to be cut to fit. The nail method, on the other hand, allows you as little or as much overlap as you need.

Where a structure abuts against a wall you must provide a run-off for rain water at the junction point. This flash could be zinc, lead or copper chased into the mortar, but a simpler alternative is to use self-adhesive flashing.

Door catches, handles and the ventilator stay add the finishing touches, along with weatherboarding, which should be nailed over the roof ends and treated with preservative.

17 *The window sill is fixed above the bottom cladding to provide a weather seal. All metal fittings must be of a type suitable for outdoor use*

Variations on the basic theme

Mini greenhouse: A smaller version of the lean-to greenhouse, this is tended from the outside and has one or more opening doors at the front. Usually, this type of greenhouse is essentially a modified lean-to in which similar methods of construction to the basic design are used, with twin doors placed centrally and no end door.

The internal height should be at least 1500mm so that shelving can be fitted to double the effective area, allowing 700mm headroom for plants on each level.

Apex or span: This is a free-standing model which rises to a central ridge and it can be constructed along the lines of two lean-tos placed back to back.

The necessary modifications include a central ridge with capping, a central door in one end, and side and end bracing to provide rigidity.

18 *One great advantage of cladding the greenhouse with PVC roof sheeting is that it can be stretched or squashed to take up minor adjustments*

19 *With the end of the roof butted against the backing wall, the joint can be made weathertight with a timber batten, mastic and self-adhesive flashing*

Arc and gas welding

The advantages of welding ● Gas and arc welding equipment ● Safety and clothing ● Setting up the welding kits ● Welding with gas ● Arc welding ● Common welding faults and their solutions ● Distorted joints and how to avoid them

Welding is one of the most commonly used metal joining processes because a welded joint is quick to make, strong, cannot be shaken loose by vibration, and may be almost invisible when it is ground down and painted over.

Like brazing and soldering, welding is a method of joining which requires plenty of heat. There are two types of welding: *arc welding,* where a high-energy spark melts the filler rod and the pieces of metal being joined so that they fuse together; and *gas welding* where an oxy-acetylene flame is used to melt the filler rod into the joint between two components.

Although mild steel is the metal most commonly welded, the process can also be adapted for metals such as copper and aluminium, but remember that you must use the correct filler rods and that you cannot weld dissimilar metals together.

In the UK oxygen and acetylene gas bottles are expensive and not easy to acquire so the DIY welder is usually confined to the use of small portable arc-welding kits which can be bought or hired surprisingly cheaply. In most other countries gas is easier to come by and, because gas welding techniques are slightly simpler, oxy-acetylene equipment is recommended for the beginner.

Equipment

In addition to the actual welding equipment, there are a number of other articles you should get from a tool or hire shop before you start any welding work. The first is a welding mask, of which there are two types: ordinary goggles with smoked lenses which are sufficient for gas welding and brazing; and a full-face mask which is necessary to protect your face and eyes from the very strong light rays given out by an electric arc.

You also need leather gauntlets to protect your hands from flying sparks and hot metal. Flame-proof cotton overalls (or, preferably, a leather apron) will protect your clothes.

You should avoid using matches to light oxy-acetylene torches as it is impossible to control the torch properly while both hands are occupied with matches and a box. Instead use a proprietary flint lighter which keeps your hand well away from the flame as it is lit, or at the very least an ordinary cigarette lighter.

Professionals use a steel table on which to carry out welding operations, but you can make do with a sheet of asbestos or a sheet of steel laid on a workbench to protect the timber from the flame or arc.

Ray Duns

Most portable arc welding kits can be plugged into an ordinary domestic socket outlet, but units with a very high current rating require their own 440 volt three-phase supply. Check with your supplier when buying or hiring one and describe the type of jobs you will be doing so that you get a unit with the correct range of current ratings.

A. Above: *Welding is not the simplest of metal joining techniques and requires the most specialized equipment, but once mastered it produces the quickest, strongest, and most efficient joints*

Gas welding

Gas welding is a technique very similar to brazing, which is described on pages

1 *When you set up a gas welding kit position the bottles next to the work and open the valves momentarily to clear out any dirt inside them*

2 *Screw the regulators into the cylinder valves, and then the gas pipes into the regulators. Oxygen pipes are colour coded blue, acetylene red*

3 *Before fitting the welding torch to the two pipes open the regulators for a second to check their operation and to purge the pipes of any impurities*

4 *Open the acetylene valve on the torch and light the gas with a cigarette lighter, then adjust the flame until it burns smokelessly at the tip*

5 *Slowly open the oxygen valve and adjust the flame until it becomes neutral: the outer cone should be pale in colour, the inner one very bright*

2246 to 2251, and you should re-read these pages before you carry on with this part of the Metalwork course.

Oxy-acetylene equipment consists of two colour-coded gas cylinders – black for oxygen, maroon for acetylene – two regulators and a welding torch. The regulators ensure that the pressure of the gas delivered to the torch is correct, regardless of the pressure inside the cylinder. The torch has interchangeable nozzles (called *tips*) with different diameters of tip orifice, the larger tips being used for thicker metals.

Setting up: Many gas welding kits are supplied with both cylinders mounted on a trolley. If yours is not, move the cylinders near to the workplace and leave them standing upright.

Clear any dust that may have settled in the cylinder valves by opening them both slightly and closing them immediately, then fit the regulators. These screw into the cylinder valves – the acetylene regulator has a left-handed thread to prevent confusion.

Make sure the regulator adjusting knobs are slightly open before opening the cylinder valves by half a turn, this being sufficient for most types of welding. As soon as these are open close the regulator valves. Now you can attach the hoses leading from the torch to the regulators – maroon to the acetylene, blue to the oxygen bottles – screwing them to the regulator outlets. Acetylene fittings have left-handed threads.

Open the regulator adjusting knobs slightly and allow the gas to blow any dust and debris out of the hoses for a few seconds before closing them and connecting the hoses to the torch. Finally close the cylinder valves and open the two valves on the torch to allow the gas to drain out of the tubing and regulator. The welding outfit is now ready to use, but remember always to allow the gas to flow through the torch for a few seconds before you light it up – this purges the hoses and torch of any impurities.

Using gas equipment
Start by 'opening up' the equipment: checking that the two torch valves are closed and the regulator valves open, open the cylinder valves half a turn, oxygen cylinder first. The acetylene cylinder valve is opened with a special spanner which should be left in place.

Open the oxygen valve on the torch and adjust the oxygen regulator until the delivery pressure is about 70 kNm^2 then

Gas welding equipment

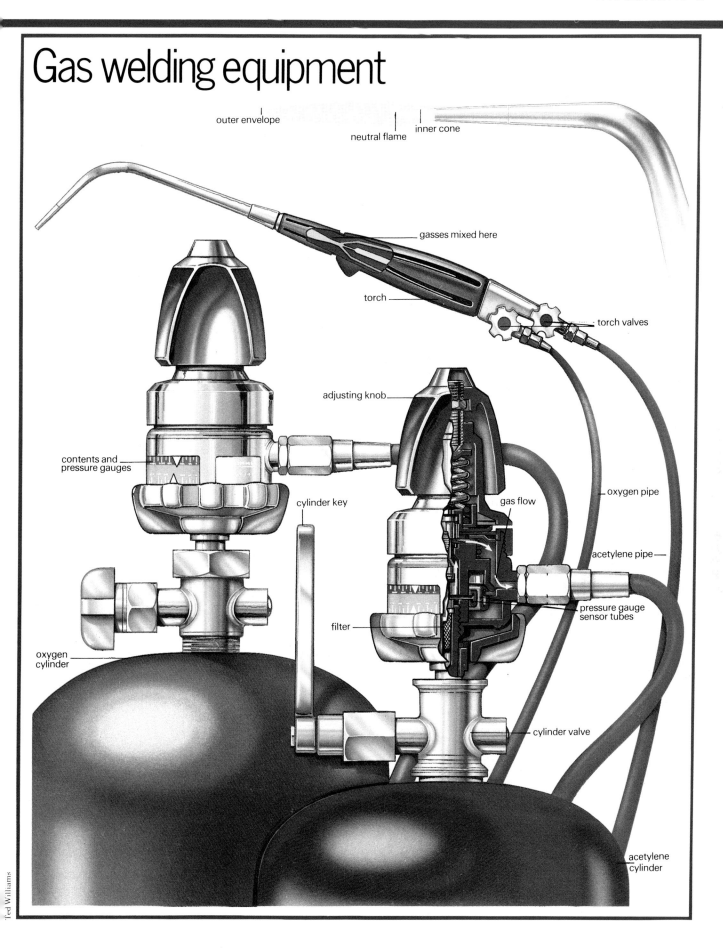

outer envelope

neutral flame

inner cone

gasses mixed here

torch

torch valves

adjusting knob

oxygen pipe

contents and pressure gauges

gas flow

cylinder key

acetylene pipe

filter

pressure gauge sensor tubes

oxygen cylinder

cylinder valve

acetylene cylinder

Ted Williams

close the torch valve and repeat this procedure with the acetylene supply.

Now, with a pair of welding goggles on your forehead, open the acetylene torch valve and light the gas. Open up the valve until you get a soot-free flame.

Place the goggles over your eyes and open the oxygen torch valve; keep doing so until the flame at the tip is *neutral*. A neutral flame is divided into two distinct zones: a sharply defined inner cone with no 'feather', and a pale nearly invisible outer cone.

Forehand welding: This is the name given to the standard welding technique, where the filler rod is moved along the joint ahead of the flame. It is a similar technique to that used in brazing (see pages 2246 to 2251), and the filler rod and torch must be kept at the correct angle all the time. The rod should be at 30° off the workpiece and the torch nozzle 60° off it so that they form a right-angle. Hold the torch so that the inner cone is about 2mm from the joint, and the filler rod so that its tip is just outside the inner cone.

With the work laid out on a welding table tack the ends of the joint together to hold the workpiece in place. Heat the joint area with the torch until it goes bright red and melts then apply the filler rod to build up the 'puddle' (see pages 2246 to 2251).

6 *Wearing gloves and goggles, and with a suitable steel or asbestos surface on which to work, you can start welding your components together*

7 *If the steel welding table absorbs too much heat and prevents a successful weld, you may have to insulate the workpiece with asbestos*

8 *For certain joints you must arrange the components on a former and tack them together before welding properly, as if you were brazing*

9 *When setting up an arc welding machine, select the correct current setting for the job before you plug it in and switch it on*

10 *Attach the clamp on the work cable to the steel work table or to the workpiece itself, making sure that a good electrical contact is made*

11 *With the machine still switched off select the correct filler rod and fix its bare end into the electrical contacts in the electrode clamp*

To make the rest of the joint carry out this procedure, moving the torch slowly along the work in a rhythmical sequence until the weld has a regular rippled pattern, stands slightly proud of the workpiece, and penetrates right through the joint.

When welding thicker sections of metal together you must leave a space between them to allow the filler to flow into the joint. This can be half the thickness of the metal sections themselves, and for sections over 3mm thick you must chamfer the edges as well—especially when you are making a butt joint.

Arc welding

Electric arc welding is by far the most common DIY welding process in the UK. In the hands of a skilled operator an arc weld can be made far more easily and quickly than a gas weld, but the techniques require a great deal of practice before a professional standard is reached.

The basis of arc welding is the high-energy spark between the electrode and workpiece which melts them both simultaneously to form a solid joint. This is achieved by the welding machine which is basically a mains transformer powered from an ordinary socket outlet. Two heavily-insulated copper cables run from this: one of them (the *work cable*) is securely clamped to the workpiece; the other to an electrically and thermally insulated clamp which holds a flux-coated electrode.

When the arc is struck the circuit is complete and electric current flows from the welding machine through the electrode and workpiece and back to the machine through the work cable. This melts the metal around the joint as well as the electrode, which melts and fills the joint so fusing the components.

Safety: In all heat-joining methods safety is of vital importance. In the case of arc welding you must consider not only the fire risk involved in the job, and the risk of hurting yourself, but the brightness of the arc itself.

This is so great that it can burn the skin and severely irritate the eyes, a condition commonly known as 'arc eye'. To protect yourself wear a leather apron and gauntlets, roll your sleeves down and wear a full-face welding mask. This is usually made of compressed fibreboard or glass-fibre with a heavily smoked lens and can either be held in one hand or worn with a headband.

Warn people near you not to watch the arc while you are working, keep inflammable materials well out of the way, and do not weld while wearing damp shoes or clothes—as otherwise you may sustain a serious shock.

Setting up: Connect the two cables to the welding machine. Run the work cable to the workpiece and clamp it firmly to both pieces being joined. If you are using a steel-topped table you can connect the clamp to this instead. Select the required type and diameter of electrode for the job you are doing by consulting the table printed on the packet in which they are supplied, and fit this to the electrode clamp by its bare end.

Most welding machines come with a data sheet giving a range of possible electric current ratings for each type of job and electrode. Where you have a selection of ratings from which to choose for your job pick the middle or average current rating and adjust the control knob on the machine to this output.

Finally, before plugging in and switching on lay the electrode down well away from the work piece and the steel welding surface. Do this at all times so that you cannot accidentally strike an arc while the machine is switched on, and switch it off when not in use.

Making the weld

You can weld components at any angle so there is no need to arrange them for an 'uphill' weld as in brazing and gas welding. Merely clean the joint faces and arrange them with the correct gap between them.

Switch on the machine and start the job by striking the arc. Tap one end of the joint with the electrode and immediately withdraw it 2-3mm to form the correct gap and get the spark (or arc) established. Do not increase the gap as oxygen and nitrogen from the atmosphere can pollute the electrode metal, giving a weak and brittle weld.

Once you have struck the arc draw the electrode along the joint holding it in line

B. *A basic arc welding kit. The technique of striking the arc to start the weld (shown below) is not difficult, but requires plenty of practice*

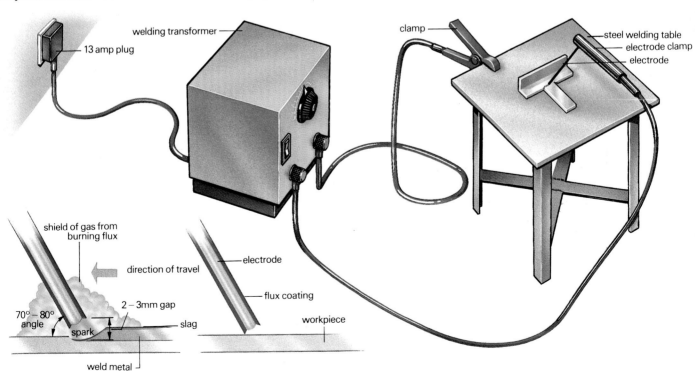

welding transformer — 13 amp plug — clamp — steel welding table — electrode clamp — electrode

shield of gas from burning flux — direction of travel — electrode — flux coating — 2–3mm gap — slag — 70°–80° angle — spark — workpiece — weld metal

with the joint but about 10-20° off the vertical. This ensures that the slag formed by the molten flux remains behind the arc and does not get trapped in the weld itself. Move the electrode along the joint at a steady rate, maintaining the gap between it and the workpiece as it burns away.

In a good weld the joint is slightly raised with a regular and close ripple pattern, and complete penetration. This may not be immediately apparent so chip away the slag when the joint has cooled to reveal the weld metal. You will have to do this in any case before painting or finishing the joint.

Welding problems: These are normally the result of one of the following errors:
● Incorrect current setting
● Incorrect welding speed
● Too great an arc gap
● Wrong electrode angle

In the first case too high a current will cause excessive welding temperatures and will burn away the workpiece, while too low a current prevents sufficient penetration and causes too much build-up. If you move the electrode across the workpiece too fast the filler does not penetrate the joint sufficiently and the weld is narrow and weak; too slowly and there is a wasteful build-up along the outside of the joint (fig. C).

12 *Switch the machine on and tack the joint at each end. Chip the slag off the tacks and run the electrode down the line of the joint*

13 *When you have finished the joint allow it to cool for a few moments and then chip the slag off the weld with a chipping or cross-pein hammer*

14 *Before painting or otherwise finishing a weld joint, clean all the slag off the weld with boiling water and a stiff wire brush*

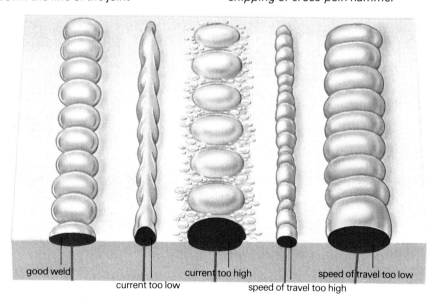

Ted Williams

good weld

current too low

current too high

speed of travel too high

speed of travel too low

C. *Arc welding faults. From the left: a perfect weld; a weld done with too low a current; one with too high a current (note the spatter beside the weld); a weld made too quickly with little penetration; and a weld made too slowly with excessive penetration and a wasteful build-up of filler*

15 *One way to counter distortion in a welded T-joint is to tack the joint on opposite sides of the T before you start welding it properly*

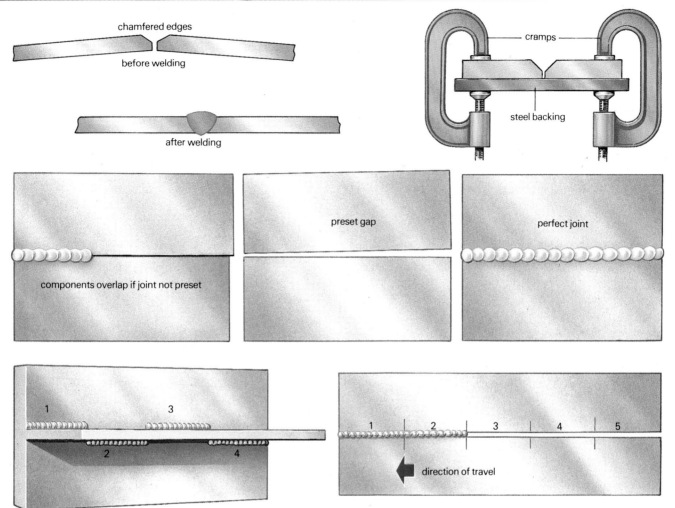

chamfered edges

before welding

after welding

cramps

steel backing

components overlap if joint not preset

preset gap

perfect joint

sequence welding

1

3

2

4

backstep welding

1

2

3

4

5

direction of travel

Ted Williams

An excessive arc gap gives a weakened joint which may not show up even when slag gets trapped in the weld. This is also a hazard if the electrode angle is wrong.

Making the joints

Welded joints in metal should be set up in the same way as brazed joints. The illustrations on pages 2246 to 2251 show a number of the most common types of joint, but note that thin sheet metal cannot be butt-welded – it must be lapped or folded before being welded.

In the case of thick metal sections you must chamfer the edges of the joint before butt-joining them, but you may also need to make several runs with the electrode or the gas welding torch to fill the joint. In this case chip the slag off the completed run, or wire brush a gas welded joint, before doing the next run of welding.

Distortion: One of the problems peculiar to welding, and due entirely to the high temperatures involved, is that of distortion. As the metal is heated along the joint, this part of it expands and causes the workpiece to twist out of

shape. It is impossible to prevent this, but it can be allowed for so that the problems are 'cancelled out'.

The simplest way to counter distortion is to tack the joint with a series of short welds along the line of the joint. Once it is secure you can weld the rest of the joint. Alternatively you can pre-set the joint: butt joints tend to 'fold' upwards slightly when welded so support the components so that the joint forms a ridge (fig. D).

In the same way you should set one end of the joint slightly wider than the other as the weld draws the two components together. Increase the gap in a butt joint by about 9mm for every 1m of joint.

Another way of avoiding distortion problems is to clamp together the components being welded. In the case of a butt joint you can do this by clamping the pieces of a stiff steel backing plate with G-cramps (fig. D). This allows the components to expand along their lengths and widths, but not to flex relative to each other. In more complex cases you must use items such as angle iron, bolts and G-cramps to hold angled joints in place.

D. *Distortion due to heat is a major problem for any welder: shown here are ways of avoiding it by careful planning*

If either of these are impossible you can try backstep welding: divide the joint into lengths of about 50mm, and weld up the section nearest one end – working from the middle out towards the end. Now weld the second section, working towards the first weld, and so on. In this way the metal will unsuccesfully try to distort towards the part of the joint already welded up (fig. D).

In the case of a T joint where you are welding on both sides of the central part of the T, divide the joint again into 50mm lengths. Weld the first 50mm of one side of the T, the second 50mm of the other side, and the third 50mm of the first, and so on. In this way you will effectively 'cancel out' the distortion that occurs when you weld one side first and then the other. You can then fill in the spaces on both sides by welding up the rest of the joint. This method will also be found useful for other complex types of joint.

A supportless shelf system

Max Logan Associates

Made from a mixture of softwood battens and man-made boards, this sleek-looking shelving system has flowing lines–and no apparent supports. The support is actually a batten concealed within the structure of the shelf

As a refreshing change from most shelving systems with their profusion of brackets and supports, why not build this good-looking design which appears to have no support at all.

Its clean flowing lines are at home in a variety of modern furnishing styles, and you can choose from any number of finishes to suit your decorative tastes and colour scheme.

Instructions are given for making the system in three different widths to suit your storage needs and the room you are fitting it in. The illustration on the left shows a living room, where it has been used to combine the functions of a sideboard or stereo tower and bookshelves. The working drawings show a layout suitable for a bedroom.

Instructions are also given for adding extra horizontals inside a dip, and there is a suggestion for adding simple drawers.

Although there is no visible support, the shelves are actually on battens–in a similar way to shelving for an alcove–but these are concealed within the thickness of the shelves. This provides a secure fixing for the back of the shelves. At the ends, a similar batten fixes them to the side walls. Because of the length, a shelf fixed only in this way would tend to sag along its front edge, and so needs further support. This is provided by periodically arranging for the shelf to have a short vertical section, forming a step and a change of level. This braces the rest of the structure and provides visual interest. As shown on the left, you can exaggerate this step and form a deep U-shape–fit shelves across it to make a very handy storage unit. Very short shelves (up to a maximum of around 500mm) which are fitted against the side wall can be straight with no change of direction, as illustrated overleaf. Otherwise, design the shelves to have a step of at least 150mm at maximum intervals of 900mm.

Before starting construction of the shelves, you must work out a suitable layout taking into account the steps and their intended uses. Plan also what widths of shelving will be needed at each point. A simple sketchplan of the room wall will make this much simpler.

When you have arrived at a suitable design, you should trace the run of each shelf on to the wall using a spirit level and a straightedge to ensure that verticals and horizontals are true. Note that it is not necessary to cut or remove skirting boards, as deep dips can be arranged to stop above them.

Following your line on the wall, screw the support battens in place, scribing them to fit where the wall is uneven. Note that the narrower shelves also use a thinner support batten. Stop the battens short of the corners as shown, to provide for fixing the corner blocks.

When all your battening is in place, you can assemble the shelves to fit on them. There are several methods of construction, depending upon the finish and style you want, but they are all similar in principle. Each is a sandwich construction in man-made boards around a frame of softwood battens. Corners and fascias are added afterwards, and you can choose these from a number of styles.

Whichever design you choose, make up a series of short sections to suit the battening. Cut out the upper board to size and assemble the battening on its underside. Then fix the underside board in place.

Try each section of shelving in place on its support batten. If the wall is uneven, you will have to scribe the back of the upper and lower board to fit.

When this has been done, you can fit each section in place, screwing through from the underside (or the inside face on verticals).

Now, make up corners from quadrant, square or triangular moulding on support blocks. Fit these in place to lock the sections together.

When the run of shelving is complete add the fascia, which can be rectangular or half-round with neat corner joints to suit the corner blocks.

If your shelf is faced with melamine, it will need no finishing other than edging strip. Otherwise, fill any gaps, sand and finish with paint.

Project

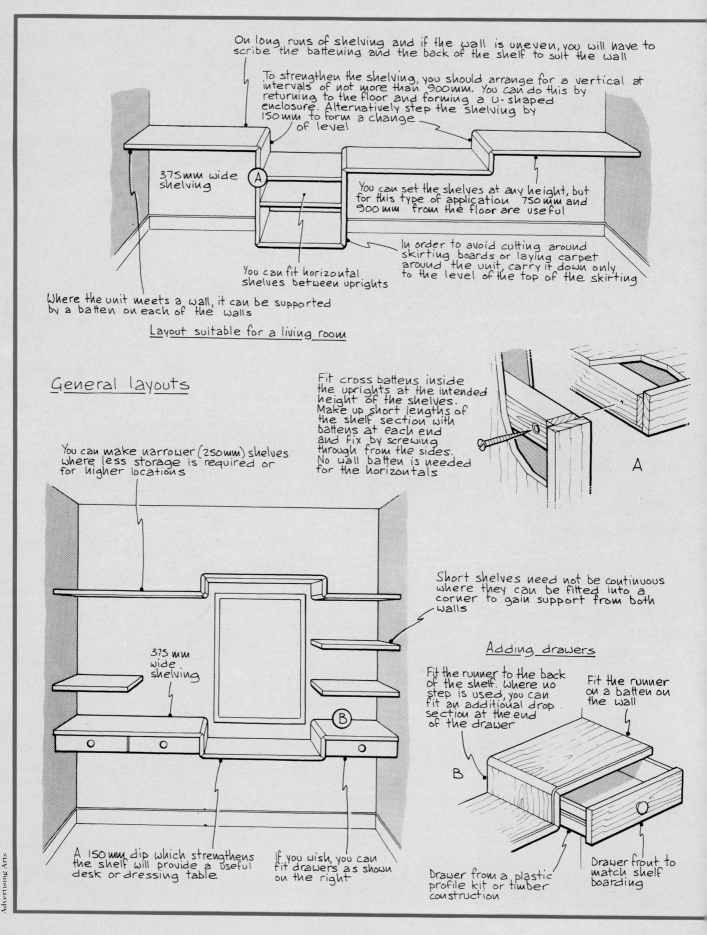

On long runs of shelving and if the wall is uneven, you will have to scribe the battening and the back of the shelf to suit the wall

To strengthen the shelving, you should arrange for a vertical at intervals of not more than 900mm. You can do this by returning to the floor and forming a U-shaped enclosure. Alternatively step the shelving by 150mm to form a change of level

375mm wide shelving

A

You can set the shelves at any height, but for this type of application 750mm and 900mm from the floor are useful

You can fit horizontal shelves between uprights

In order to avoid cutting around skirting boards or laying carpet around the unit, carry it down only to the level of the top of the skirting

Where the unit meets a wall, it can be supported by a batten on each of the walls

Layout suitable for a living room

General layouts

You can make narrower (250mm) shelves where less storage is required or for higher locations

Fit cross battens inside the uprights at the intended height of the shelves. Make up short lengths of the shelf section with battens at each end and fix by screwing through from the sides. No wall batten is needed for the horizontals

A

375 mm wide shelving

Short shelves need not be continuous where they can be fitted into a corner to gain support from both walls

Adding drawers

Fit the runner to the back of the shelf. Where no step is used, you can fit an additional drop section at the end of the drawer

Fit the runner on a batten on the wall

B

B

A 150mm dip which strengthens the shelf will provide a useful desk or dressing table

If you wish, you can fit drawers as shown on the right

Drawer from a plastic profile kit or timber construction

Drawer front to match shelf boarding

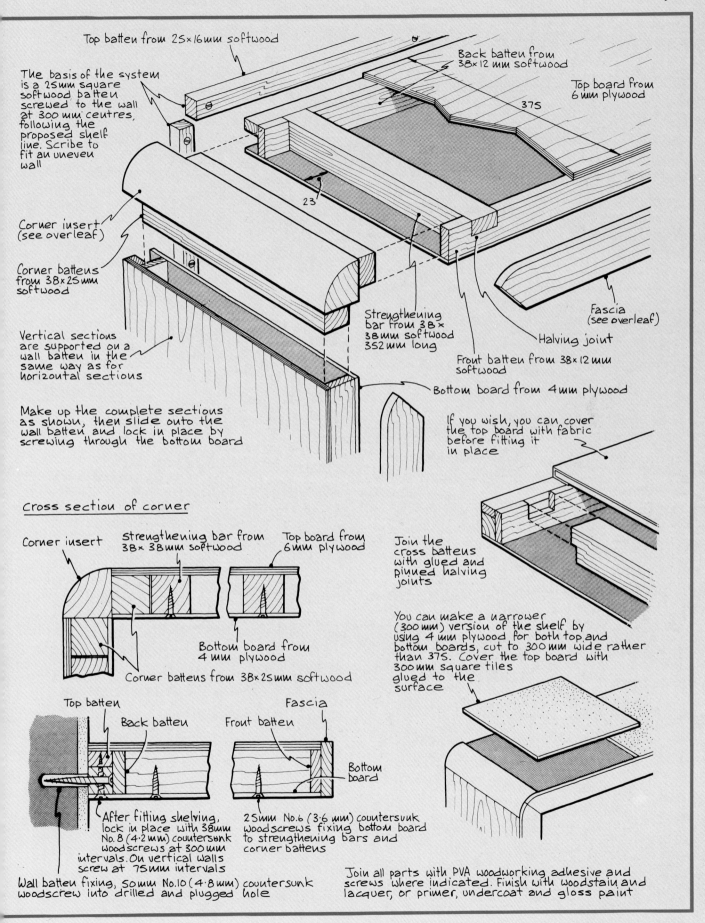

Top batten from 25×16mm softwood

Back batten from 38×12mm softwood

Top board from 6mm plywood

The basis of the system is a 25mm square softwood batten screwed to the wall at 300mm centres, following the proposed shelf line. Scribe to fit an uneven wall

375

23

Corner insert (see overleaf)

Corner battens from 38×25mm softwood

Strengthening bar from 38×38mm softwood 352mm long

Fascia (see overleaf)

Halving joint

Front batten from 38×12mm softwood

Vertical sections are supported on a wall batten in the same way as for horizontal sections

Bottom board from 4mm plywood

Make up the complete sections as shown, then slide onto the wall batten and lock in place by screwing through the bottom board

If you wish, you can cover the top board with fabric before fitting it in place

Cross section of corner

Corner insert

strengthening bar from 38×38mm softwood

Top board from 6mm plywood

Join the cross battens with glued and pinned halving joints

Bottom board from 4mm plywood

Corner battens from 38×25mm softwood

You can make a narrower (300mm) version of the shelf by using 4mm plywood for both top and bottom boards, cut to 300mm wide rather than 375. Cover the top board with 300mm square tiles glued to the surface

Top batten

Back batten

Fascia

Front batten

Bottom board

After fitting shelving, lock in place with 38mm No.8 (4·2mm) countersunk woodscrews at 300mm intervals. On vertical walls screw at 75mm intervals

25mm No.6 (3·6mm) countersunk woodscrews fixing bottom board to strengthening bars and corner battens

Join all parts with PVA woodworking adhesive and screws where indicated. Finish with woodstain and lacquer, or primer, undercoat and gloss paint

Wall batten fixing, 50mm No.10 (4·8mm) countersunk woodscrew into drilled and plugged hole

Project

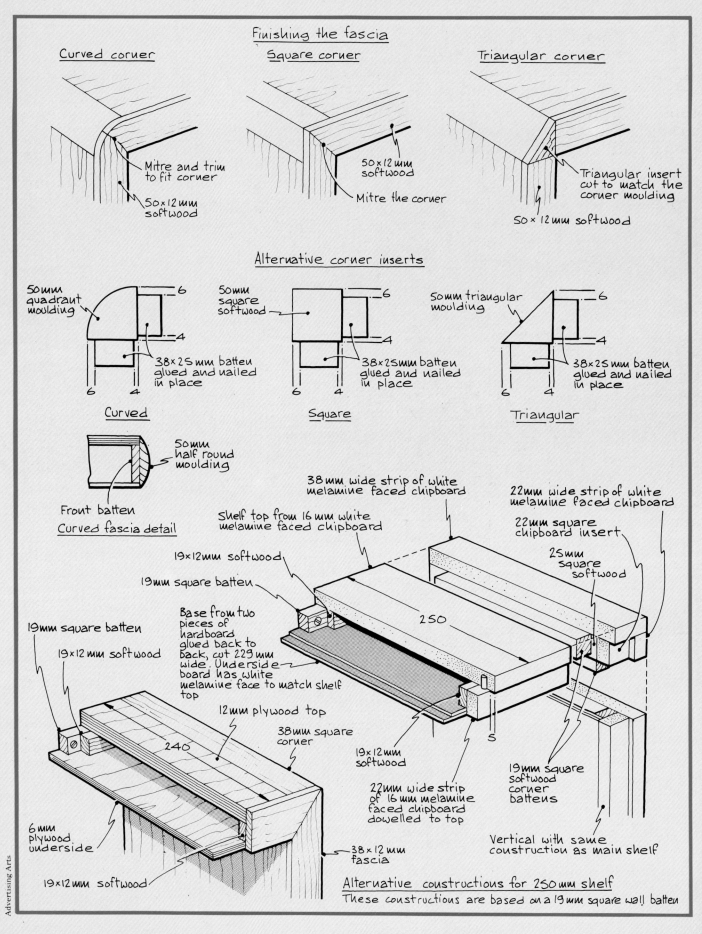

Finishing the fascia

Curved corner

Mitre and trim to fit corner

50 x 12 mm softwood

Square corner

50 x 12 mm softwood

Mitre the corner

Triangular corner

Triangular insert cut to match the corner moulding

50 x 12 mm softwood

Alternative corner inserts

50 mm quadrant moulding

6

4

38 x 25 mm batten glued and nailed in place

6   4

Curved

50 mm square softwood

6

4

38 x 25 mm batten glued and nailed in place

6   4

Square

50 mm triangular moulding

6

4

38 x 25 mm batten glued and nailed in place

6   4

Triangular

50 mm half round moulding

Front batten

Curved fascia detail

38 mm wide strip of white melamine faced chipboard

22 mm wide strip of white melamine faced chipboard

Shelf top from 16 mm white melamine faced chipboard

22 mm square chipboard insert

19 x 12 mm softwood

25 mm square softwood

19 mm square batten

Base from two pieces of hardboard glued back to back, cut 229 mm wide. Underside board has white melamine face to match shelf top

250

19 mm square batten

19 x 12 mm softwood

12 mm plywood top

38 mm square corner

240

19 x 12 mm softwood

5

6 mm plywood underside

22 mm wide strip of 16 mm melamine faced chipboard dowelled to top

19 x 12 mm softwood

19 mm square softwood corner battens

Vertical with same construction as main shelf

19 x 12 mm softwood

38 x 12 mm fascia

Alternative constructions for 250 mm shelf
These constructions are based on a 19 mm square wall batten

Advertising Arts

2420

Herb gardens

A herb garden cleverly combines practicality with beauty. As well as their famed culinary and medicinal uses, herbs also provide an attractive array of shape and colour and fill the air with a delightful aroma of mixed scents

Below: *A delightful outdoor herb garden in the classic style. The planting looks informal but in fact has been done with care so that colours and shapes contrast with the higher plants at the back. The herbs themselves include aromatic and medicinal, as well as culinary, examples*

A herb garden can be as large and complex or as small and simple as you like, depending on the amount of space you want to allow for it and how you choose to organize it. In a large garden, for instance, you can create a separate, formal herb garden, laid out in a traditional pattern. While in smaller gardens, the herbs can be intermingled with borders of flowers and vegetables for a decorative effect.

Even on a patio, pots and troughs planted with a selection of aromatic herbs make a delightful and unusual addition. A wide selection of herbs can be grown in pots indoors and in window boxes, so even if you have no garden at all, you can still enjoy the pleasure of fresh herbs.

Growing herbs indoors
A sunny window sill in the kitchen is the most practical place for growing herbs indoors. The fresh leaves are immediately available to the cook and the green plants themselves provide a welcome and apt addition to the decor. Some herbs, such as parsley, tarragon and winter savory, are attractive enough not to seem unduly out of place when grouped with more conventional pot plants.

Not all herbs are suitable for indoor cultivation but many of the most commonly used and best known will thrive in pots. Some herbs, including parsley, dill and basil, can be raised from seed in the late summer, preferably outdoors, and then transferred to pots inside for autumn and winter supplies. (Herbs cannot be raised from seed indoors during the winter.)

Other herbs, such as marjoram, sage, rosemary, mint and chives, are best grown from cuttings or divisions taken in the autumn. However, even perennials will not last forever indoors, and to

Iris Hardwick Library

Above: *Some herbs in constant use – like this mint – can be grown indoors in water. Fill your chosen pot with pebbles for the roots to grip*

for expensive, custom-made stone troughs. These old sinks can often be found in secondhand and junk shops and they are more commonly used for growing alpines and rock plants.

The sink can be left in its natural state or be camouflaged to create an attractive 'stone' container. Mix together one part sand, one part cement and two parts peat then add enough water to give a stiff consistency. Coat the outside of the sink with a strong adhesive and leave until tacky. Spread the prepared mixture over the adhesive, using a trowel, and leave the surface as it is to simulate stone.

When the coating is dry, cover the drainage hole with crocks and fill the container with fairly rich garden soil or a good compost. Suitable herbs for growing in a sink garden include borage, summer savory, sage, mint, basil and parsley.

Below: *The kitchen window is an ideal place to grow culinary herbs and places them right at your fingertips. You can use pots – as here – or a window box*

ensure a constant supply, it is best to take fresh cuttings each year.

Use a good potting compost and crock the pots well to allow for drainage. It is a good idea to stand the pots on moist gravel in a shallow tray to keep the soil from drying out. Then simply water the plants regularly and keep them away from draughts.

Patio and window boxes
The range of herbs which can be grown in containers outdoors is much larger. As most of them are renowned for their fine foliage – some bear colourful and rather pretty flowers – they can create an eye-catching display.

Virtually any kind of container is suitable for growing herbs, with the exception of hanging baskets. Individual pots in appropriate sizes can be used for herbs such as lemon balm, caraway, dill, coriander, chervil, sage and marjoram. Larger plants, such as bay trees, can be grown in tubs.

Special parsley pots are particularly attractive and can also be used indoors. These are tall, cylindrical, terracotta pots with a series of openings in the sides through which individual plants grow.

A miniature herb garden planted in a window box or trough is not only decorative but, with careful planning, can provide almost all your culinary needs. Old-fashioned glazed sinks provide a cheap and practical substitute

To take full advantage of their aromatic leaves, plant some thyme in between paving stones on the patio. Whenever the leaves are stepped on, they will release the most pleasant smell.

Herb borders

Herbs grow very successfully intermingled with other garden plants. Their cultivation requirements are fairly undemanding and they need little in the way of special treatment. They prefer a sunny position and will grow well on most soils, but do best on a light, well-drained, alkaline soil. A single application of a general all-purpose fertilizer in spring and a light topdressing of lime in autumn will keep them in good condition. Follow the same general rules for planting, thinning, watering and so on, as you would for other biennials and perennials.

Low-growing and spreading herbs are ideal for planting in this way, but take care that they are not overshadowed by taller plants. Lemon thyme, tarragon, mint and other herbs which spread very rapidly are excellent in beds planted with tall flowers as they quickly provide weed-suppressing ground cover. In fact, they

Below: *Antique or unusual containers like this wooden wheelbarrow provide the ideal planting ground for herbs on a patio or terrace*

spread so easily and so fast that you may need to surround them with slates or some other form of barrier sunk in the soil to prevent them overrunning and strangling neighbouring plants.

Herbs planted among vegetables add colour and beauty to this less attractive part of the garden. An especially good combination is the classic culinary mixture of basil and tomatoes. Not only is this very convenient for harvesting, but basil is reputed to keep away black fly.

Here again, you can take advantage of the sweet scent of the leaves by planting sage or thyme in the borders beside a lawn. In this way, whenever you mow the lawn, the bruised leaves of the herbs will yield an enchanting aroma.

A formal herb garden

A formally arranged herb garden offers immense decorative opportunities to the creative gardener as well as plenty of scope to the imaginative cook. A wide range of herbs can be grown, including some of the more unusual ones such as caraway, lovage, fennel, angelica, horse-radish and cumin. In addition, you can plant some of the more decorative varieties of common herbs, such as variegated sage and golden thyme.

A gently sloping site in a sheltered part of the garden is ideal. Herbs do best in warm, still air so, to provide protection

and to delineate the area, it is a good idea to surround the herb garden with a hedge. Rosemary is both pretty and practical for this purpose, otherwise lavender and sage are good alternatives. There are a number of traditional methods for laying out a herb garden and there are numerous other possibilities too. Before you start, however, it is well worth planning the beds and their contents in detail on paper first. Bear in mind such factors as the amount of space available, the heights of the plants, the juxtaposition of colours, paths and means of access.

There are three basic approaches popularly used for planting a herb garden. It can be botanically orientated, planned thematically or designed purely for visual beauty.

The botanic approach has been favoured in many public gardens but may not be fully satisfying for the amateur gardener. The aim is to grow a comprehensive collection of herbs arranged in their natural order. Each bed is devoted to one order of plants and includes a wide range of individual specimens. This method requires a lot of space, however, and may not be practical if you simply want a good supply of herbs for cooking.

The thematic approach is very much a matter of personal taste and requirements. For example, you could confine

Iris Hardwick Library

Above: *Low walling around a patio or roof garden can be topped with boxes of herbs to provide a delightful aroma as well as a decorative touch*
Below: *Another good place for a herb garden is a flower bed in the middle of a lawn. For the best effect, try to vary the sizes and colours of the plants*

your choice entirely to one type of herb, such as medicinal. Alternatively, you might plant several separate beds each containing a different type – one culinary, one medicinal, one aromatic and one flowering.

Famous thematic herb gardens have been created on the basis of growing only those herbs mentioned in the Bible or in the works of Shakespeare. Some have been recreations of mediaeval, monastic gardens while others have the herbs arranged to spell out a name or message.

A herb garden designed solely for its visual appeal is, perhaps, the most delightful and rewarding of all. The beds are shaped to form a pattern, such as a chessboard or a spoked wheel. The herbs are then planted with the deliberate intention of displaying the most pleasing combinations of colour.

The chessboard pattern is very popular and fairly easy to do. Prepare small, square beds in staggered rows for the herbs. Strictly speaking there should be 32 squares, but absolute accuracy is not essential. Either pave the spaces in between to create the 'white' squares of the board, or sow them with camomile. Afterwards plant a different herb in each of the other beds.

Other patterns, such as the wheel, are rather more ambitious and require very careful planning, preparation and measuring of shaped beds and paths. Often a central focal feature, such as a sundial or statue, is incorporated to enhance the overall effect.

An indoor herb garden

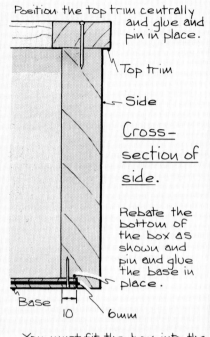

Position the top trim centrally and glue and pin in place.

Top trim

Side

Cross-section of side.

Rebate the bottom of the box as shown and pin and glue the base in place.

Base
10   6mm

You must fit the box into the reveal far enough from the window so that it does not interfere with opening it. If the sill is not wide enough or you need extra support, make up wooden brackets as shown.

125

Bracket from 150 x 25mm PAR softwood.

Shape to a smooth curve.

Screw holes for wall mounting.

Screw and glue the brackets to the batten with two 50mm Nº.8 (4·2mm) countersunk woodscrews.

Support batten 150mm long from 50 x 25mm PAR softwood.

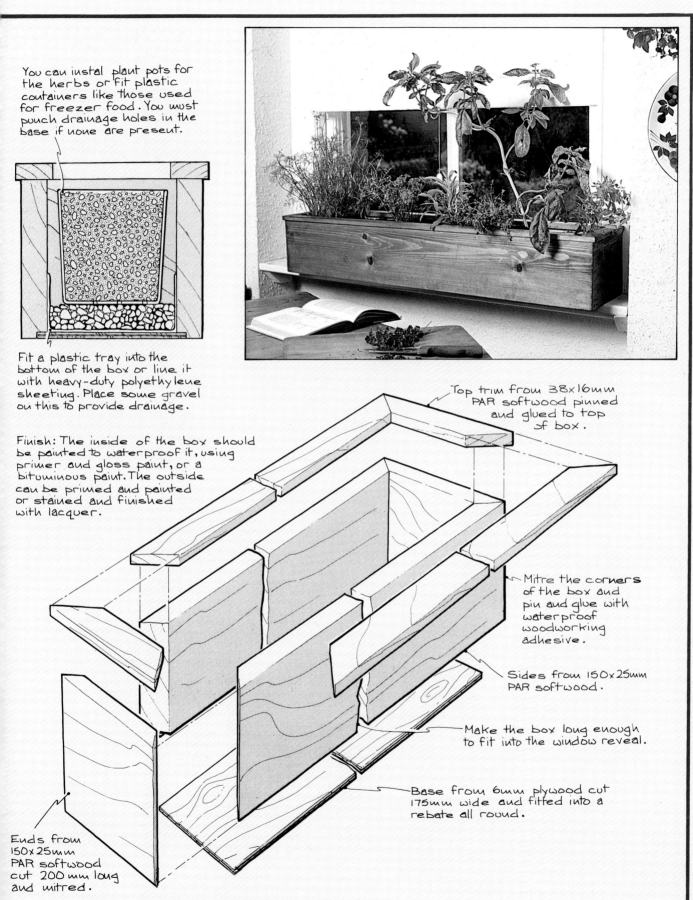

You can instal plant pots for the herbs or fit plastic containers like those used for freezer food. You must punch drainage holes in the base if none are present.

Fit a plastic tray into the bottom of the box or line it with heavy-duty polyethylene sheeting. Place some gravel on this to provide drainage.

Finish: The inside of the box should be painted to waterproof it, using primer and gloss paint, or a bituminous paint. The outside can be primed and painted or stained and finished with lacquer.

Top trim from 38x16mm PAR softwood pinned and glued to top of box.

Mitre the corners of the box and pin and glue with waterproof woodworking adhesive.

Sides from 150x25mm PAR softwood.

Make the box long enough to fit into the window reveal.

Base from 6mm plywood cut 175mm wide and fitted into a rebate all round.

Ends from 150x25mm PAR softwood cut 200 mm long and mitred.

Advertising Arts

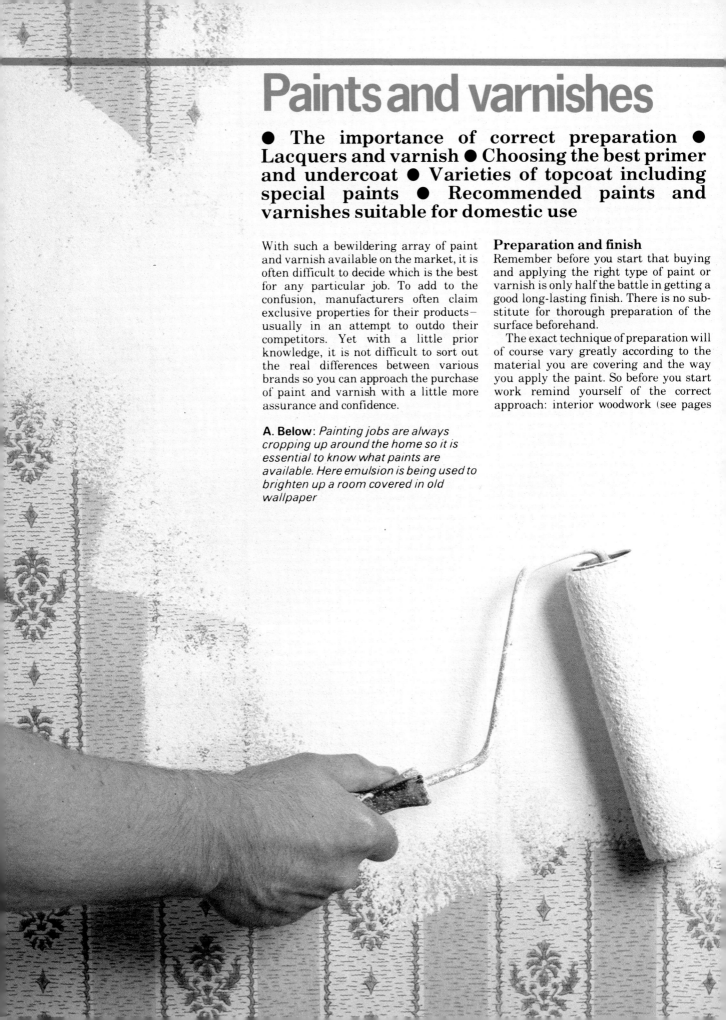

Paints and varnishes

● The importance of correct preparation ● Lacquers and varnish ● Choosing the best primer and undercoat ● Varieties of topcoat including special paints ● Recommended paints and varnishes suitable for domestic use

With such a bewildering array of paint and varnish available on the market, it is often difficult to decide which is the best for any particular job. To add to the confusion, manufacturers often claim exclusive properties for their products— usually in an attempt to outdo their competitors. Yet with a little prior knowledge, it is not difficult to sort out the real differences between various brands so you can approach the purchase of paint and varnish with a little more assurance and confidence.

A. Below: *Painting jobs are always cropping up around the home so it is essential to know what paints are available. Here emulsion is being used to brighten up a room covered in old wallpaper*

Preparation and finish

Remember before you start that buying and applying the right type of paint or varnish is only half the battle in getting a good long-lasting finish. There is no substitute for thorough preparation of the surface beforehand.

The exact technique of preparation will of course vary greatly according to the material you are covering and the way you apply the paint. So before you start work remind yourself of the correct approach: interior woodwork (see pages

1 *The first step when painting timber is to prime the bare wood. For most jobs a universal primer—usually white in colour—is used*

2 *Lead-based primers are usually pink in colour. Use these with extreme care and avoid getting any of the paint anywhere near your mouth*

3 *For high quality work on timber which is resinous or on areas subject to extreme wear and tear, use aluminium wood primer*

110 to 115); walls and ceilings (see pages 430 to 435); exterior wood and metal (see pages 542 to 546); texture painting (see pages 677 to 683); outside walls (see pages 1189 to 1192); and spraypainting (see pages 1264 to 1267 and 1308 to 1312). It is also important to use good quality painting tools—particularly brushes—and to keep them in perfect condition (see pages 1341 to 1347). And remember that even with the best tools and materials painting defects can often occur because the method of application is wrong (see pages 1892 to 1896).

Lacquers and varnish

The term 'varnish' is a widely accepted term used to describe all types of transparent paint applied to wood. Yet strictly speaking not all transparent paints are varnishes. Many are more correctly described as 'lacquers' since they dry by a combination of solvent evaporation and chemical action and not just by evaporation of the solvent as is the case with varnish. In terms of finish there is not really a lot of difference between varnish and lacquer, although many lacquers are polyurethane based which gives them a tough resilient surface.

Varnish and lacquers are available in a variety of finishes—gloss, silk (semi-gloss) and matt—some for interior use, others specially designed for use out of doors. Most are 'one-pack' (in one tin) but for sealing floors and other areas which require a tough and long-lasting finish, you can use a 'two-pack' varnish or lacquer with a separate catalyst which needs to be added just before use. For traditional finishes—particularly on furniture—special spirit-based varnishes are produced as well as shellac lacquers, French polish and button polish (see pages 1318 to 1322).

Usually no special primers or undercoats are necessary when applying varnish or lacquer; two or three coats of the sealer should be perfectly adequate. For a very fine finish leave the undercoats to dry thoroughly and then rub down each coat with a piece of fine glasspaper or wire wool before applying the final coat.

Primers and sealers

The purpose of primer/sealers is to treat bare surfaces—unpainted metal or new timber, for instance—and seal them before applying an undercoat and topcoat. Without such treatment subsequent coats would eventually peel off or in extreme cases refuse to stick properly in the first place.

General purpose primer: This oil-based paint will perform well on both bare wood and metal, and is the one you should use unless you require a special treatment (see below).

Alkali-resistant primer: This is used to seal masonry surfaces before applying spirit or oil-based paints. With this primer it is a good idea not to rub down the surface before applying the next coat as this could break the seal.

Alkali-resistant primers also tend to bind floury or flaking surfaces but if this is a severe problem you should use a *stabilizing primer* instead.

Aluminium wood primer: Do not be fooled by the name: this is not aluminium paint, nor is it for priming aluminium surfaces. Instead it is a high quality toughened primer which has good sealing qualities particularly on resinous or sticky timber surfaces.

Lead primer: This is the traditional primer for bare wood or metal and is usually pink in colour. It is now rarely used (except for galvanized metal) since

4 *Universal metal primer (often known as zinc chromate primer) is ideal for all ferrous metals as well as aluminium and metal alloys*

modern substitutes have rendered it unnecessary. If you need to use a lead-based primer remember that it can constitute a health hazard and should be applied with care. Try to avoid getting the paint anywhere near your mouth and wear a face mask if you need to sand it down. Even when the primer has dried hard it can still be a danger to young children or animals who might chew or lick the surface, so try to apply an undercoat and topcoat to cover it up as soon as possible.

Metal primers: Apart from general purpose primers there are a number of primers designed especially for metal surfaces. The most common is *universal metal primer* (often known as zinc chromate primer). This is yellow in colour and is ideal for all ferrous metals as well as aluminium and metal alloys. It is a good rust inhibitor even in particularly

5 Before painting masonry surfaces it is wise to apply an alkali-resistant primer. On flaky surfaces use a stabilizing primer

6 Following this, exterior walls should be given two or more coats of masonry or cement paint. Both are available in a variety of different colours

7 Use a roller fitted with an extension pole when painting external walls. This greatly speeds up the job and avoids wear and tear on brushes

8 When tackling downpipes and gutters make sure that any areas of bare metal around fixings are primed before coating with bitumen paint

Ray Duns

9 Interior topcoats are available in a number of different finishes: gloss (used here), matt, semi-matt, satin and eggshell

Dulux

damp climates or regions near the sea. Another common metal primer, *calcium plumbate*, is intended for galvanized iron only. This contains lead so it should be used with extreme care (see above).

Undercoats

The purpose of an undercoat is to provide a smooth surface for subsequent coats. A good undercoat should therefore not only cover the surface but also fill out any small bumps and irregularities—particularly around corners and edges where the paint tends to rub thin.

Undercoats can be either spirit or water-based. Spirit-based paint gives good overall coverage but dries out fairly slowly and needs to be left for at least 24 hours before the topcoat can be applied. Water-based (acrylic) undercoats dry hard within two or three hours so you can apply the topcoat on the same day.

Water and spirit-based primer/undercoats are also available. These save a great deal of time by allowing you to prime and undercoat all in one go. They are suitable for most materials although bare metal (or screw and nail heads) should be treated with a good quality metal primer first. Exceptionally porous surfaces may need a spirit-based primer first to seal the surface before application of an undercoat or primer/undercoat.

Topcoat paints

These are the most common of all the grades of paint since they are used both when you are renewing the surface coating or painting it for the first time. Inside, a topcoat has to look attractive and provide adequate protection against accidental knocks, possible staining, and changes in temperature and humidity. Outside its primary function must be to

withstand the vagaries of the weather and to protect the exterior of the house.

Topcoats may be applied over old paint surfaces or on top of newly painted undercoats or primer/undercoats (see above). Which of these techniques you employ will depend on the type and condition of the surface to be covered (the substrate) as well as the variety of topcoat you are using. Often only one topcoat needs to be applied, in other cases two or even more may be necessary.

Emulsion: This is the most popular topcoat for walls and ceilings; indeed, for interior brick and plaster it is practically the only type of paint you can apply. The pigment which gives the paint its colour is suspended in a water base. Once the paint is applied the water evaporates leaving a thin layer of pigment on the surface being covered.

Some types of emulsion have additives which greatly improve their quality so look for these before buying. Those containing *vinyl* or *acrylic* for instance, will be far tougher than ordinary emulsions and the surface can be washed down without risk of the paint dropping off in the process.

The main advantage of using emulsion is that it is easy to work with and apply; there is little 'drag' on the brush or roller compared with oil-based paints (see below). Cleaning tools and brushes is also relatively easy; all you need to do is wash them down in a bucket of clean lukewarm water. And compared with other surface coverings emulsions are relatively cheap so you can cover a large area—such as a wall or ceiling—inexpensively.

Emulsions can be applied to a wide variety of surfaces including asbestos, plaster, brick, render and stucco; it can even be used to seal over old bitumen paint. More importantly, it can be applied

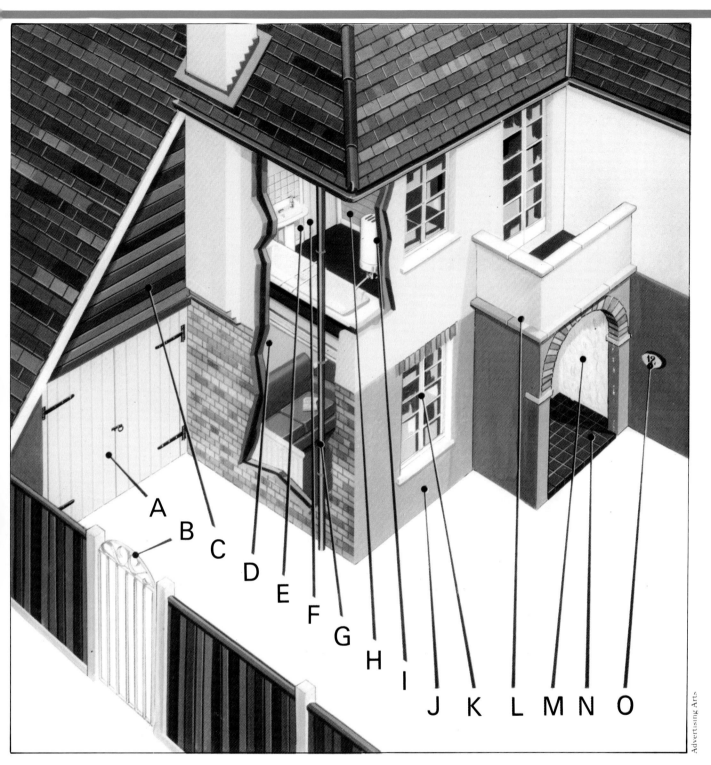

A B C D E F G H I J K L M N O

B. Above: *Paints and varnishes suitable for various parts of the home.*
A. *Exterior paintwork – good quality primer and undercoat followed by a 'hardglaze' or polyurethane topcoat.*
B. *Metal gates and other metallic surfaces – universal or lead primer with an oil-based topcoat.* **C.** *Exterior timber – to retain the natural wood effect use two or more coats of exterior grade polyurethane lacquer.* **D.** *Interior walls*

and ceilings – emulsion, matt or silk finish. **E.** *Interior paintwork – primer, undercoat and topcoat all with oil-based paint.* **G.** *Downpipes and gutters – bituminous paint.* **H.** *Steamy kitchens and bathrooms – protect walls and ceilings with anti-condensation paint.* **I.** *Around boilers and fireplaces – heat-resistant paint.* **J.** *Exterior walls – masonry or cement paint.* **K.** *Metal window frames – universal metal*

primer or lead primer with oil-based paint suitable for metal. **L.** *Damp patches on interior and exterior walls – coat with damp-proof paint or anti-fungus paint.* **M.** *Cracked or bumpy walls and ceilings – texture paint.* **N.** *Door steps, tiled areas and brickwork – red tile paint.* **Q.** *Name plates and house numbers – lettering picked out in oil-based paint; the sign is then covered in two or more coats of polyurethane lacquer*

10 *Interior surfaces which are subject to continued wear and tear – such as cupboard doors – should be coated with a hard gloss paint*

11 *Emulsion is the most popular topcoat for interior walls and ceilings. It can be applied easily and quickly using a roller and paint tray*

12 *Small or awkward areas are better tackled using a brush. If more than one coat is needed, thin down the first coat with a little water*

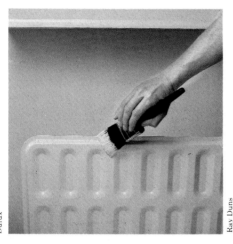

16 *Central heating radiators can be covered with emulsion or oil-based paint – but remember that light shades will discolour easily*

17 *Red tile paint can be used on brickwork and masonry as well as tiled areas. It is particularly popular for doorsteps and tiled window ledges*

18 *A spray gun is ideal for almost all types of oil or water-based paint but it must be used with care or – as shown here – the paint will run*

to these surfaces directly, without any undercoat or primer. And if more than one coat is needed – on a porous surface, for example – the first coat can be thinned down with a little water before it is applied.

Two further characteristics of emulsion paint make it perfect for some types of building material. Since it is alkali-resistant it can be used on surfaces – such as cement, bricks and certain fillers – which have a high alkali content. Many other types of paint would adhere to these materials for a short time and then peel off. Emulsion paint also has the advantage of being permeable. This means that it does not 'seal off' the background surface like many other paints but allows it to 'breathe'. Because of this you can use emulsion on relatively new plaster before it has fully dried out.

Useful as it is, emulsion paint does have some distinct disadvantages. It is generally only available in matt or silk so if you want a high gloss finish you have to use an oil-based paint. Also, despite additives such as acrylic and vinyl, emulsion paint is not particularly tough. The surface is easily chipped or damaged by accidental knocks, contact with hot items or even by people constantly brushing past certain areas.

Textured paint: This is a heavy-bodied paint which can be applied to walls and ceilings and then textured into various patterns using combs, sponges and other tools (see pages 677 to 683). It is available either ready-mixed or in powder form.

As well as brightening up an otherwise dull wall or ceiling, textured paint is particularly useful for covering and disguising cracked or bumpy surfaces. Of course, large indents and badly broken or damaged plaster cannot be disguised or

made good, but if the damage is minimal then textured paint may be the solution.

One word of warning. If you decide to use textured paint try to choose a pattern that you can live with since the material is extremely difficult to remove without damage to the background.

Outdoor wall paint: Ordinary emulsion paint is not really suitable for outside walls since it is far too easily damaged and will in time be washed off. It is far better to use a paint specially designed for outdoor use.

Two types are available. The most popular variety – known as *masonry paint* – is similar in appearance to emulsion. What makes it different is the addition of small particles of mica, quartz, sand and nylon fibre to the paint to give it body and strength. This means that it will last much longer than ordinary emulsion, although the

13 *Alternatively, coat walls and ceilings with texture paint. This consists of a thick compound which can be formed into a variety of patterns*

14 *Swirl effects are one of the most popular texture patterns. These are inscribed on walls and ceilings using a special brush with rubber bristles*

15 *Heat-resistant paint withstands temperatures well in excess of 200°C. It is useful for painting pipework, and areas around boilers and fireplaces*

strengthening material does tend to wear out brushes and other tools far more quickly than other paints. Like emulsion, masonry paint is permeable and alkali-resistant and splashes can easily be washed off with water providing they are not allowed to dry hard.

An alternative for outdoor walls is *cement paint,* which is sold in powder form and should be added to water before being used. It is available in white and in a variety of shades including the more traditional masonry colours.

Cement paint has the advantage of being cheap but it is not as durable as masonry paint. And although it can be applied on top of practically all un-decorated surfaces (except gypsum plaster) it cannot be painted directly on to other coatings.

Wood and metal paint: Unlike water-based emulsions these are usually oil or spirit-based. They are available in a number of finishes: gloss, matt, semi-matt, satin or eggshell.

Wood and metal paints are extremely resilient and will withstand knocks, or repeated scrubbing, rain and even temperature and humidity changes. Yet they are certainly more difficult to apply than other paints since the brush tends to 'drag' over the surface and you have to take quite a lot of care to get an even coat without runs or sags. Unlike emulsions they cannot be applied directly to an unpainted surface but only on top of old paint or on an undercoat. Yet they do have the advantage that they can be used on almost any surface, providing it is prepared correctly beforehand.

Manufacturers spend a great deal of effort and money trying to improve the quality of oil and spirit-based paints. One way they have done this is by mixing additives to the paint, and it is well worth

looking for these before buying. One of the most common additives, *thixotropes,* gives the paint a jelly-like consistency so that it does not drip off the brush or sag when applied to the surface. This also means that the paint requires less 'brushing out' so that you need only apply one coat instead of two or three. These paints are normally known as 'non-drip'. Another additive is *brush wash.* This allows you to clean tools and equipment in water instead of using either a proprietary brush cleaner or white spirit.

Perhaps the most useful additive is *polyurethane resin.* This makes the paint more hardwearing although it does marginally reduce its glossiness.

Special topcoats

There are a huge range of special paints which have relevance for home use and most are available from large builder's merchants and hardware stores.

Anti-condensation paint: This can be used on all interior surfaces which suffer from condensation and is particularly useful in kitchens and bathrooms. The paint has an insulating substance – such as cork flour – added to it to 'warm up' the background surface and stop condensation forming.

The paint is available for masonry surfaces, wood and metal. It dries to a matt, slightly textured finish and can be covered with a further topcoat, if desired, without reducing the effectiveness of the original paint in any way.

Anti-fungus paint: If you have fungal growth on interior walls the best solution is to find the cause of the problem and to cure it at source (see pages 789 to 793 and 1229 to 1233). But an anti-fungus paint may cure minor growths or at least be used as a back up measure. Before you apply the paint remove the existing

fungus with a wire brush and sterilize the wall with a bleach solution.

Bituminous paint: This is probably the most widely used special paint. It has extremely good weather-resistant properties, but because it is not very attractive its use is usually confined to areas where looks do not matter – such as the inside of gutters, metal roofs and storage or garden sheds.

Bitumen will dissolve many other paint solvents so if you want to paint over the top you should first seal the surface. Try to keep a special brush for use only with bitumen in case you contaminate other paints.

The most durable type of bitumen is black; coloured bitumens are more attractive but wear out too quickly and soften in the heat. If you want to paint the inside of a galvanized cold water storage cistern you should use a special, non-tainting bitumen paint.

Damp-proofing paint: A *silicone paint* or *emulsion bitumen treatment* will not cure damp walls but will help check it for a period of time. The best solution is of course to instal a proper damp-proof course or membrane to cure the problem (see pages 710 to 717).

Fire-retardant paint: Fire-retardant paint is particularly useful in areas where there is a potential fire risk. This and other fire precautions are dealt with in detail further on in the course.

Heat-resistant paint: Paints are available which can withstand temperatures well in excess of 200°C. These are especially useful around boilers or fireplaces. If you want to paint central heating radiators, heat resistant paint is not usually necessary; use a normal oil-based paint or emulsion but remember that light shades – particularly brilliant white gloss – will discolour easily.

Redesigning the bathroom –1

- **Causes of dissatisfaction** ● **Relieving congestion** ● **Planning a layout** ● **Plumbing** ● **Relocating drainage** ● **Curing condensation** ● **Buying bathroom furniture** ● **Space requirements for bathroom appliances** ● **Two bathrooms redesigned**

A. Left: *Redesigning a bathroom requires careful planning due to the expense and the scale of plumbing work involved. Approached carefully, however, a major conversion can add more than its cost to the overall value of your house*

This two part series on bathroom renovation takes an in-depth look at the roots of dissatisfaction with your existing bathroom facilities and provides a number of ideas and solutions to common bathroom problems. Redesigning a bathroom is not something that should be undertaken lightly, not only because it is likely to lead to considerable expense, but also because once the work has been done there is little you can easily do should you be unhappy with the results.

The key to successfully redesigning the bathroom therefore lies primarily in the planning stages and in the correct assessment of your particular problems. This is the subject of this article, while the second part of the series deals with

B. Below: *When laying out your bathroom consider the amount of space each piece of equipment needs: shown here are the basic requirements of a bath, bidet, WC, and a fully-enclosed shower cabinet*

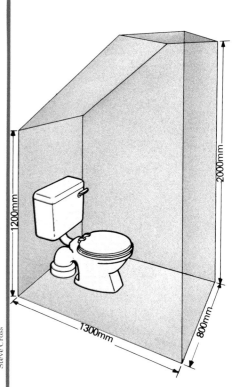

2000mm

1200mm

1300mm

800mm

the actual work involved in fitting new units and plumbing them in.

Unless all you need is some form of cosmetic renovation—simple redecoration, or perhaps fitting new tiles—you will find that there are four main categories of bathroom problems: congestion; layouts; fittings; and condensation or cold. All too often a single room combines all four, but if you consider each of the problem areas carefully, you may find that solving one may make the others far easier to deal with later on.

Congestion

When too many people want to use the bathroom at the same time, this can be a major source of family friction. The best solution here is to see whether it is possible to provide extra facilities elsewhere in the house so that the whole family does not have to rely on access to a single bathroom.

Remember that a small WC and hand basin can be accommodated in a space as small as 1300mm × 800mm, so even if you are not fortunate enough to live in a large house you may be able to find room for such a project. Although a WC must always have washing facilities nearby, this need not be a problem as plenty of tiny basins are available—you can even get triangular ones designed to fit into a corner. The main restrictions concern the proximity of suitable soil and waste drainage pipes, and proper ventilation will also have to be provided (see below).

Elizabeth Whiting

C. Above: *The apparent size of this small bathroom has been increased by removing the WC and by using white paint on the walls. Concealed lighting and extra storage space add to the effect*

If you find that you can instal a separate WC elsewhere in the house, and your bathroom is very small, it is worth considering removing the existing WC and making space for a shower or bidet. The only real disadvantage in not having a WC in the bathroom is that, for families with babies, this is the ideal place for changing nappies.

Pressure on single bathrooms can also be relieved by installing wash basins in one or more bedrooms. This solution is particularly effective if some members of the household exclude others from the bathroom by lengthy make-up and hair washing sessions. Wherever possible, instal new basins where they will get maximum use. Remember that inset vanity basins can quite easily be installed in a worktop or cupboard.

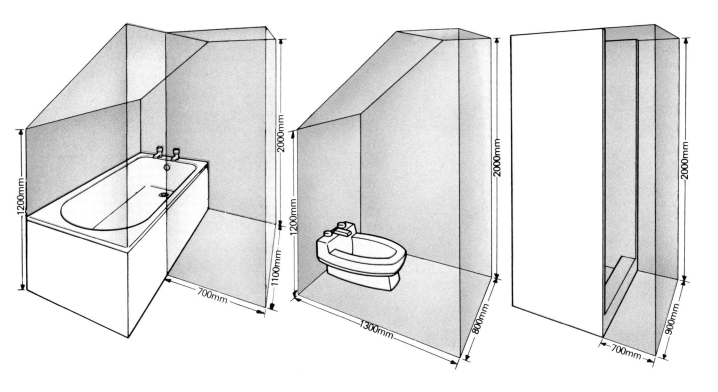

Elizabeth Whiting

D. Above: *Cheap but chic: painted brick walls and minimal ornamentation have made this attic into a useful second bathroom for very little cost*

Alternatively, you can cut down on the time that each person spends in the bathroom by installing – and encouraging the use of – a shower. These have the added advantage of using less water than a bath, and even if space or your budget excludes the possibility of fitting a separate shower, you can easily convert your present bath by fitting new taps with an integral shower attachment. A completely separate shower room, including a hand basin, needs only 1600mm × 900mm of space, and you may find that it is worth reducing the size of a large bedroom to instal one.

Layouts

Inappropriate overall design is the second area for dissatisfaction, and this can often be improved in all but the very smallest bathrooms. The two main considerations that dictate the layout are the plumbing system and the need to provide sufficient space around the various fixtures for them to be used comfortably. Otherwise, the only considerations are the positions of the windows and doors.

Use the following guidelines to help you to design a new layout.

Drainage: The first priority in drainage planning is the location of the WC as this must be close to a soil stack or drain. If you wish to move an upstairs WC it will probably be necessary to instal a new soil stack, and whereas this is perfectly possible, it is an expensive option (see pages 728 to 732). The location of ground floor WCs is less restricted as they are usually connected directly to a drain via an underground bend; but you should keep the unit next to the outside wall near the manhole cover as laying new drains beneath floors in the house is very disruptive and also expensive.

The waste pipes for the other fittings can often be run round one or more sides

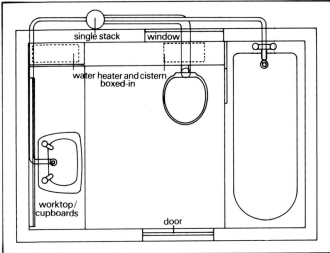

E. **Above**: *A basic but not uncomfortable bathroom. The colour scheme, badly positioned basin and inefficient use of available space offer plenty of scope for an attractive conversion*

of the room as they tend to be small diameter, but the ideal is always to aim for short pipe runs with as few bends as possible. All pipes connecting the wastes to a waste stack, combined soil/waste stack or drain (usually via a sub-stack) should slope gently downwards at the right gradients (see pages 300 to 305).

In the UK any alterations to drainage systems must be approved by the local authority, and in Australia, all such work must be entrusted to a licensed tradesman, so in either case you should check in advance that your proposed plans are acceptable.

Ventilation: Regulations in the UK about general bathroom ventilation stipulate minimum standards—either by opening windows or by mechanical means (such as an extractor fan). There are also regulations concerning the ventilation of WCs, and if you are considering installing a new WC elsewhere in the house, it is essential that you check with your local building inspector that your proposals meet the minimum standards.

Plumbing: The positions of the various washing facilities in the bathroom are influenced to a degree by the supply pipes for hot and cold water. Long runs of hot water pipe are not only unsightly, but also waste energy, so these should be avoided if at all possible. In a low pressure plumbing system the priority for cold water pipes is to get a sufficient head of pressure by ensuring that the tank is placed high enough above the taps. This is usually only a problem in a flat or attic in which a shower is installed. There should be a minimum of 1200mm

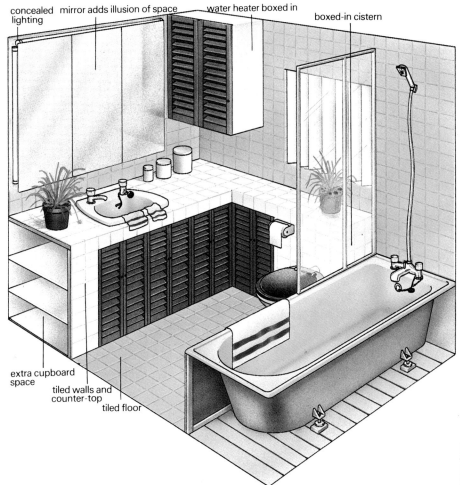

between the draw off point of the cold water tank and the shower outlet. Where this is not possible, an electric pump can be fitted to boost the pressure.

Space planning: One of the major considerations in bathroom design is the space that is provided around the various fittings. If the bathroom is to be comfortable to use, you must allow sufficient area, but remember that the minimum

F. **Top right**: *A ground plan of one possible—and very simple—conversion*

G. **Above**: *A sketch of the conversion showing how the basin has been moved and boxed in to create far more storage space. All surfaces are easy-to-clean tiles, and the wall-mounted water heater is enclosed. Although the WC cistern is also boxed in, it has not been moved and no extra plumbing is necessary*

H. Above: *A separate bathroom and WC in an old house. Both rooms are cramped, the appliances are awkwardly placed, and the plumbing and wiring (except the bathroom tumbler switch) obsolete*

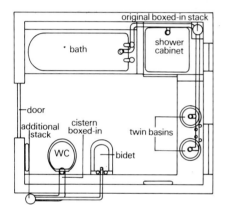

I. *A ground plan of one possible conversion. WC and bathroom have been made into one, the positions of the bath and WC interchanged, and a new soil stack installed inside the house*

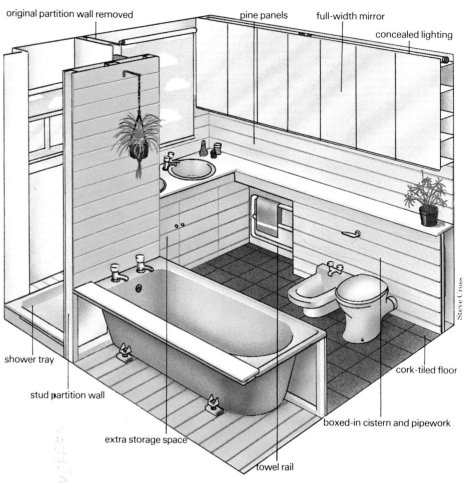

J. Above: *A sketch of the conversion showing how the new large room now accommodates a bidet and a shower cabinet with its own window. Cork tiles on the floor and timber panels on the walls aid insulation and the mirrors above the boxed-in WC cistern add to the feeling of space*

adjacent floor areas given in fig. B can overlap if the bathroom is only likely to be used by one person at a time, as is often the case.

The really crucial area is around the basin where there must be at least 200mm elbow room on either side and 700mm of space in front to allow comfortable washing. Showers with walls on one or two sides need a clear floor space of 400mm next to the tray for access and dressing, while those enclosed on three sides require 700mm in front.

Make sure that you have easy access to bath taps, and a minimum space of 700mm × 1100mm next to the bath for climbing out and drying. Where children have to be supervised the more space next to the bath the better, and a stool or covered WC pan provides a useful seat for adults or for babies being dried.

If no shower is to be fitted to the bath and you do not intend standing up in it, you can position the bath below a sloping ceiling with just enough headroom to get in and sit down (fig. B). 1200mm headroom above the base of the bath is usually adequate, but check the space beforehand by going through the actions.

In the same way – and as long as there are no problems with drainage – you can fit a WC into a space with restricted headroom (for example below stairs, or under the eaves in a top floor room). 2000mm headroom is needed to stand in front of the pan, but the roofline can slope down to 1200mm behind the cistern (fig. B). Clear space of 600mm × 800mm should be left in front of the WC for access. A bidet requires similar space above and in front, plus 200mm knee space either side (fig. B).

Windows and doors: Try to avoid placing the bath next to a window as this will make opening the window difficult and will leave bathers prone to draughts. If you find that it is not possible to avoid such an arrangement, double-glazing the window will improve conditions (see pages 453 and 502). However, this may improve insulation at the expense of good ventilation and care will have to be taken if condensation is to be avoided.

Where there is a choice, avoid having the door opening to give a direct view of the WC in case it is accidentally left unlocked by the occupant. When rearranging fittings, ensure that enough space is left for the door to swing open and for a person to step into the room and shut the door comfortably. If necessary doors can be rehung to open outwards (see pages 705 to 709) but take care that they will not hit anyone passing outside if opened suddenly.

If there is a real space problem with the door, non-standard doors may provide the solution. 600mm is an adequate width for either a bathroom or a WC. Sliding doors save space, but they are difficult to soundproof and can be awkward to use unless very carefully installed.

Fixtures and fittings

The third category of problems centres on unsatisfactory fittings, but before replacing everything in sight, make sure that the real cause of your dissatisfaction is with the design or condition of the fittings and not with the layout. Repositioning fittings is far cheaper than replacing them, so before investing in a new suite, plan your layout using the guidelines given above. However stylish a new suite, if it does not fit the available space to best advantage the bathroom will probably look better, but will certainly not work better.

Decide on the layout first as the choice of good fittings is much wider than the choice of good layouts. And when you come to choose new fittings, bear in mind that these are likely to be changed far less frequently than furniture and decorations, so take care over your choice of colour and design. Currently fashionable shapes and colours may look hopelessly outdated in 10 years time. Vast ranges of bathroom fittings are now available, varying in design, materials, colour and—inevitably—cost. The only way that you can make a good choice is by visiting a specialist bathroom showroom, or by studying the sales literature of all the major manufacturers. Take your time over your final choice, because a new suite represents a substantial investment. Also, check that the fittings of your choice satisfy local authority plumbing and drainage regulations.

K. Below: *A large and spacious bathroom which combines attractive pine panelling with the warmth of mosaic patterned vinyl sheet on the floor and bath wall*

Elizabeth Whiting

Condor Public Relations Ltd

L. Above: *Baths can be fitted into awkwardly-shaped rooms like this one, which uses cork tiles and murals to relieve the oppressiveness of a low ceiling*

Condensation/cold

A permanent solution to the problems that fall into this fourth category requires a careful analysis of existing conditions. Good ventilation and some form of permanent background heating are essential to cope with condensation caused by hot vapour-laden air meeting cold surfaces. Improved insulation and appropriate wall coverings help but are not sufficient alone.

Good ventilation will remove moisture-laden air but at the same time replace warm air with cold. A ventilation system should therefore be variable and windows should be capable of being opened wide for steamy conditions and left slightly ajar at other times. An alternative is to instal a mechanical air extraction system; as mentioned above, UK regulations make this mandatory in windowless rooms.

Space heating is a good precaution against excessive condensation, but it is important to remember that walls and ceilings can be kept far below a room temperature suitable for people and still help to alleviate condensation problems. So for fuel economy it is best to have a background source to warm the structure plus a supplementary source which can be switched on when the room is in use.

Bathrooms are often neglected when general heating for the house is being considered but they should be capable of being made warmer than the rest of the house. If you already have central heating it is simplest to add another radiator to the existing system—either to increase the comfort conditions of your present bathroom or when installing a separate shower room. However, this has the disadvantage that in summer when the heating is switched off there is no way of warming towels. It may be better to plumb-in a radiator or heated towel rail to the hot water system if the cylinder is near the bathroom (see pages 1470 to 1475). Alternatively, you could fit an electrically heated oil-filled radiator which would be sufficient to heat a smaller room.

Wall-mounted electric fan heaters or tubular radiant heaters are less satisfactory as they can only warm the room effectively if they are switched on some time in advance.

Good insulation of walls and roofs is essential, and is particularly important in older houses. If the bathroom is in an attic or on an outside wall, poor insulation frequently contributes to condensation. The insulation of brick walls can be improved by fixing foil-backed plasterboard to softwood battens screwed to the wall to leave a 25mm to 50mm air space, and roofs can be insulated by fitting glass fibre insulation quilt between the rafters and covering it with foil-backed plasterboard. The foil is essential as it prevents moisture from reaching the quilt.

M. Above: *Despite a limited budget and lack of space, creative use of cheerful colours and accessories can transform even the pokiest bathroom*

Elizabeth Whiting

N. Above: *Imaginative use of an older cellar: walls, ceiling, and steps have all been plastered and painted, and the old skylights still provide some daylight*

O. Left: *A converted bedroom in an old cottage. The chimney breast is still a major feature while the inverted dormer window subtly illuminates the bath*

Adding a cork or timber finish to the walls or ceilings also improves the insulation value. Alternatively, use polystyrene ceiling tiles for insulation, but make sure that those you choose are designed to withstand damp conditions.

Other considerations

The four categories described above are the main problem areas to be investigated when redesigning a bathroom. However, there are some further considerations to think about before any final decisions can be taken.

Careful planning of the lighting in your bathroom can make a tremendous difference to the finished effect. The most critical area is the shaving or make-up mirror which should ideally be lit so that no part of the face is in shadows. The common arrangement of a strip light above the mirror only illuminates the top half of the face – but if you find that this is the only alternative open to you, make sure that the light is at least 500mm long.

The ideal of an arrangement similar to those used in theatrical dressing rooms in which there are rows of incandescent bulbs all round the mirror is, unfortunately, unsuitable – water splashing on the

bulbs could cause them to shatter. The best alternative is to have a strip light down each side. Alternatively, spotlights can be positioned so that they shine on the face, but in this case you have to ensure that the lights are not so close that they can be adjusted by anyone standing at the basin with wet hands.

Mirror lights may be sufficient to illuminate a small room, but if a supplementary source is required, ensure that it

P. Below: *Space efficiency in a family house: the cupboard under the stairs makes an ideal second WC and shower room to take the load off the bathroom*

does not reflect in the mirror and cause glare. In the UK, remember that light switches should be of the pull cord type in the bathroom.

Storage: Another area in which you can improve the appearance and convenience of your bathroom is in the storage facilities. The basic rule is to store items nearest to their point of use—nothing is more irritating than having to climb out of the bath dripping wet to fetch a forgotten shampoo bottle.

Collecting a litter of accessories around the rim of the bath is no solution as this makes cleaning difficult and bottles can get knocked off too easily. For the bath

the ideal solution is to provide a long narrow shelf about 100mm wide running the length of the bath and at least 500mm above it. Not all layouts can accommodate this but there is usually space for some shelving within easy reach.

Other useful storage can be made by boxing-in fixtures such as the basin (see pages 684 to 687). Shelving underneath is always useful, and the counter top around the basin can accommodate frequently used bottles and containers.

Medicines are traditionally kept in bathrooms but they must be kept out of reach of children. Make sure that any medicine cabinet has child-proof locks.

A nest of tables

Drawing on a traditional design, this set of three nesting tables is perfect for occasional use and looks good on show. Like the furniture of the past, it is made from solid hardwood

Like many furniture pieces which have a long history, the nest of tables is still a practical concept. Designed to blend in with traditional furnishing schemes, this design is made from hardwood and finished with French polish for a real period feel.

All the wood used is utile – the cheapest and most readily available mahogany substitute – but any other hardwood may be employed instead. Although four different sections are specified, you need only buy two sizes as all parts except the legs can be cut from 100mm × 15mm boards.

All three frames are identical except for size. Cut the legs to length and shape them as shown. Add the rails, which are all mortise-and-tenoned in place. Note that there is no lower front rail, to allow the frames to fit together.

The tops are all made from four boards loose-tongued together. Trace out the shapes of the tops and cut them out. You can use a router to give an attractive moulded edge. Fix to the frames with metal shrinkage plates.

Fred Mancini

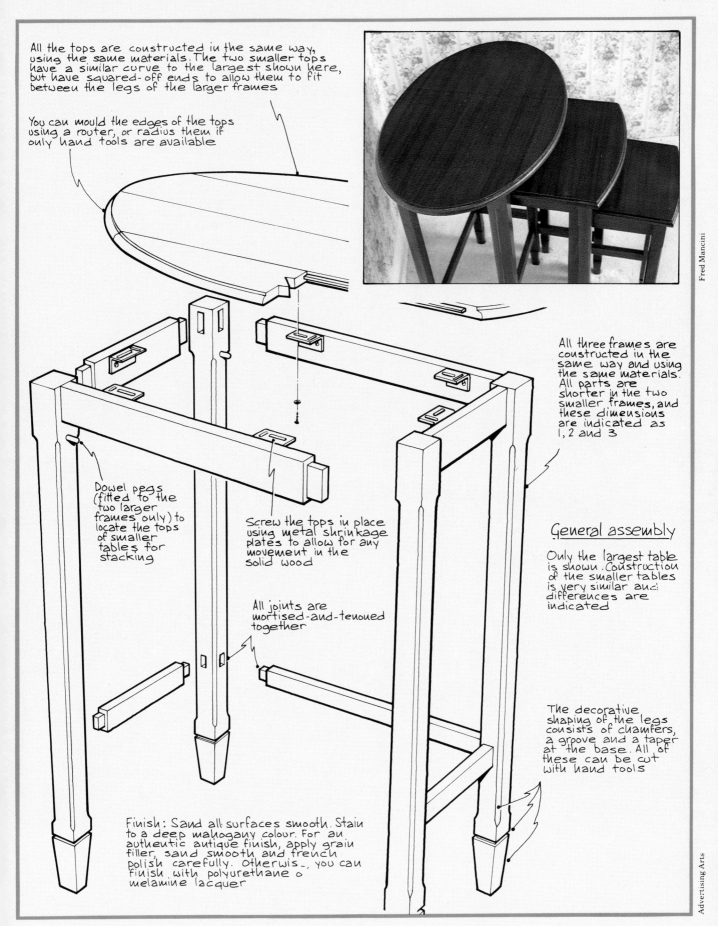

All the tops are constructed in the same way, using the same materials. The two smaller tops have a similar curve to the largest shown here, but have squared-off ends to allow them to fit between the legs of the larger frames

You can mould the edges of the tops using a router, or radius them if only hand tools are available

All three frames are constructed in the same way and using the same materials. All parts are shorter in the two smaller frames, and these dimensions are indicated as 1, 2 and 3

Dowel pegs (fitted to the two larger frames only) to locate the tops of smaller tables for stacking

Screw the tops in place using metal shrinkage plates to allow for any movement in the solid wood

General assembly

Only the largest table is shown. Construction of the smaller tables is very similar and differences are indicated

All joints are mortised-and-tenoned together

The decorative shaping of the legs consists of chamfers, a groove and a taper at the base. All of these can be cut with hand tools

Finish: Sand all surfaces smooth. Stain to a deep mahogany colour. For an authentic antique finish, apply grain filler, sand smooth and french polish carefully. Otherwise, you can finish with polyurethane or melamine lacquer

Fred Mancini

Advertising Arts

Project

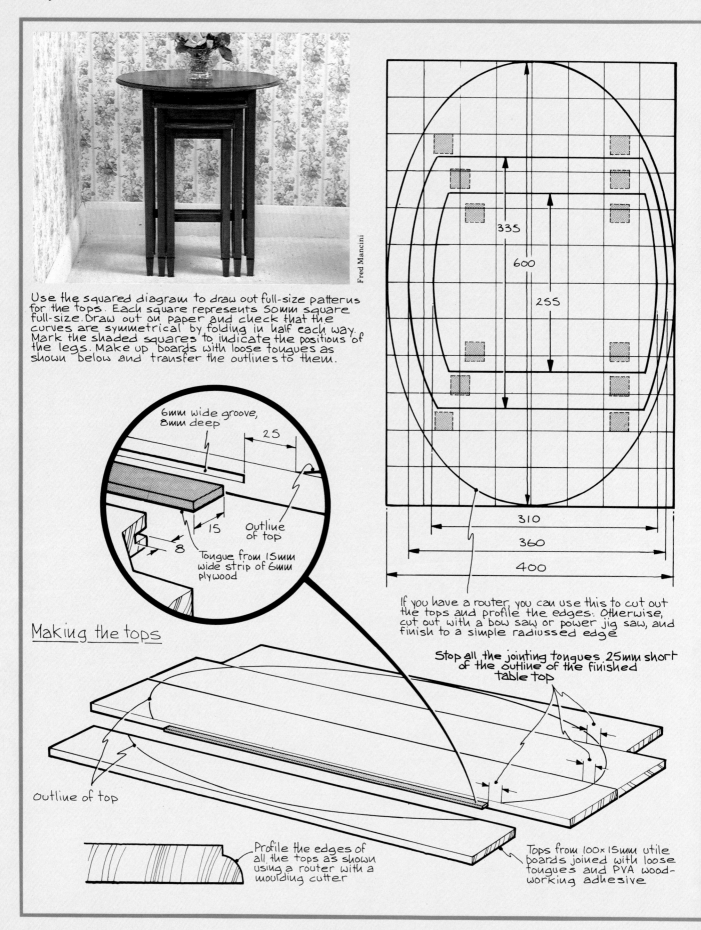

Fred Mancini

Use the squared diagram to draw out full-size patterns
for the tops. Each square represents 50mm square
full-size. Draw out on paper and check that the
curves are symmetrical by folding in half each way.
Mark the shaded squares to indicate the positions of
the legs. Make up boards with loose tongues as
shown below and transfer the outlines to them.

6mm wide groove,
8mm deep

25

15

8

Outline
of top

Tongue from 15mm
wide strip of 6mm
plywood

335

600

255

310

360

400

If you have a router, you can use this to cut out
the tops and profile the edges. Otherwise,
cut out with a bow saw or power jig saw, and
finish to a simple radiussed edge

Making the tops

Stop all the jointing tongues 25mm short
of the outline of the finished
table top

outline of top

Profile the edges of
all the tops as shown
using a router with a
moulding cutter

Tops from 100x15mm utile
boards joined with loose
tongues and PVA wood-
working adhesive

2442

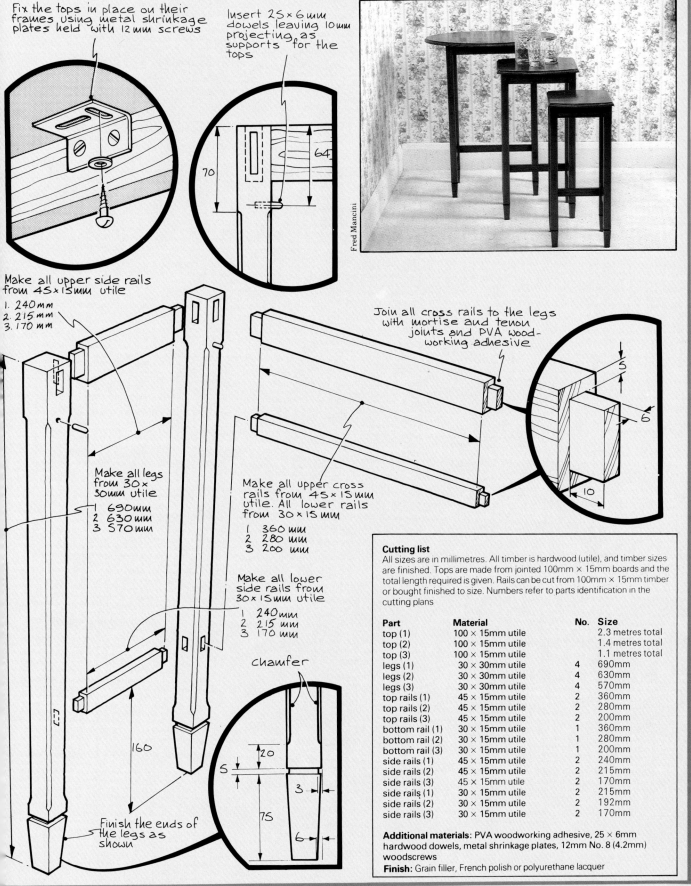

Fix the tops in place on their frames using metal shrinkage plates held with 12mm screws

Insert 25 × 6mm dowels leaving 10mm projecting as supports for the tops

70

64

Make all upper side rails from 45 × 15mm utile
1. 240mm
2. 215mm
3. 170mm

Join all cross rails to the legs with mortise and tenon joints and PVA wood-working adhesive

5

6

10

Make all legs from 30 × 30mm utile
1 690mm
2 630mm
3 570mm

Make all upper cross rails from 45 × 15mm utile. All lower rails from 30 × 15mm
1 360mm
2 280mm
3 200mm

Make all lower side rails from 30 × 15mm utile
1 240mm
2 215mm
3 170mm

chamfer

160

Finish the ends of the legs as shown

5   20

3

75

6

Cutting list

Cutting list
All sizes are in millimetres. All timber is hardwood (utile), and timber sizes are finished. Tops are made from jointed 100mm × 15mm boards and the total length required is given. Rails can be cut from 100mm × 15mm timber or bought finished to size. Numbers refer to parts identification in the cutting plans

Part	Material	No.	Size
top (1)	100 × 15mm utile		2.3 metres total
top (2)	100 × 15mm utile		1.4 metres total
top (3)	100 × 15mm utile		1.1 metres total
legs (1)	30 × 30mm utile	4	690mm
legs (2)	30 × 30mm utile	4	630mm
legs (3)	30 × 30mm utile	4	570mm
top rails (1)	45 × 15mm utile	2	360mm
top rails (2)	45 × 15mm utile	2	280mm
top rails (3)	45 × 15mm utile	2	200mm
bottom rail (1)	30 × 15mm utile	1	360mm
bottom rail (2)	30 × 15mm utile	1	280mm
bottom rail (3)	30 × 15mm utile	1	200mm
side rails (1)	45 × 15mm utile	2	240mm
side rails (2)	45 × 15mm utile	2	215mm
side rails (3)	45 × 15mm utile	2	170mm
side rails (1)	30 × 15mm utile	2	215mm
side rails (2)	30 × 15mm utile	2	192mm
side rails (3)	30 × 15mm utile	2	170mm

Additional materials: PVA woodworking adhesive, 25 × 6mm hardwood dowels, metal shrinkage plates, 12mm No. 8 (4.2mm) woodscrews
Finish: Grain filler, French polish or polyurethane lacquer

Chain link fencing

● The advantages of chain link fencing ● Types of fencing mesh ● Planning and preparation ● Digging post-holes ● Erecting fence posts and bracing struts ● Fixing the support wires and mesh ● Steel and concrete fence posts

1 Dig holes for the fence posts, fit the posts, and pack them out with stones so that they are all sunk to the same depth along the run

Chain link fencing may not be the most attractive of fencing methods, but it is robust, practical, and secure—good reasons why it has become widely used all around the world.

The practical uses of chain link fencing are almost limitless: fences of various heights can be used to keep dogs and children safely in (or out of) your garden; as a burglar deterrent; and even as a climbing frame for some popular garden plants. Whatever use you intend to put it to, chain link fencing is easy to erect, although you may need the help of an assistant for certain parts of the job.

Materials

There is a wide choice of chain link mesh types, most of which can be used with either concrete, timber, or steel fence posts. When buying your fencing materials find out from your supplier exactly what is available and what most suits your needs. All the different types of fence are erected in much the same way.

A series of fence posts are erected first and support wires slung between them at

A. Five different types of mesh. From the left they are: decorative mesh; welded mesh; a decorative welded mesh; chicken wire; and chain link. Decorative mesh is usually self-supporting

various heights to support the mesh. When the mesh is erected this is secured to the first post in a run, and then stretched between each subsequent post where it is attached to them and wire-locked to the support wires.

Chain link netting: This is often sold as a package complete with the necessary fence posts and support wires for a given length of run. The netting is available in lengths of between 10m and 50m, and in widths varying from 300mm to 3.6m. The gauge of wire used in the mesh is variable, as is the fineness of the mesh itself. For general purposes 45mm or 50mm mesh made from 11 gauge wire should suffice.

You can buy the mesh with a galvanized or aluminium-coated finish, but the most durable and attractive finish is plastic coating which is available in a variety of colours of which dark green is the most popular.

Welded mesh: This is similar to chain link mesh. Because each intersection in the mesh is welded the material is stiffer and stronger, but also more difficult to work with and more expensive. Although not so widely available as chain link mesh, welded mesh can be bought with a variety of finishes and mesh sizes.

Chicken wire: Also known as wire netting, this is much lighter than chain

link or welded mesh, and is only suitable for lightweight fencing. Because it is weaker it requires more horizontal wires to support it, although you can also staple it to a post-and-frame fence.

Decorative mesh: This is limited in range and function. The most widely available is woven picket which is a hoop-topped interlocking design of plastic-coated light gauge wire. It comes in 10-25m lengths and ranges from 250mm to 900mm in width, but however it is erected (and some types are self-supporting) it is really only suitable for decoration.

Planning and preparation

Before you start work check any pertinent building regulations with your local authority: in some circumstances you may need planning permission to erect a fence. And if the fence is to form a

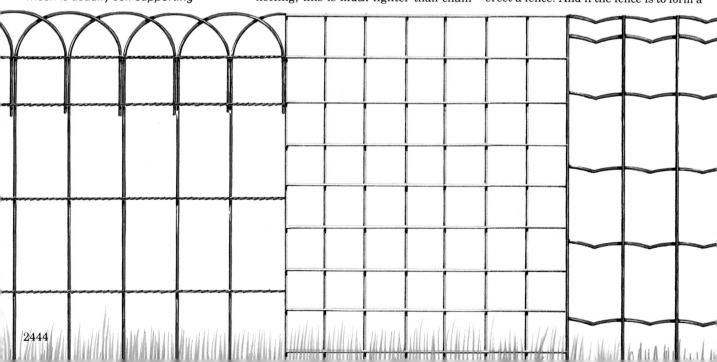

2 When you have dug holes for all the posts and any angled bracing struts, fill the post-holes with a dry concrete mix and tamp this down

3 With very light fence posts like these chestnut stakes you can chamfer the end of the bracing strut rather than cut notches in the straining post

4 Fit temporary struts to keep the posts upright while the concrete is setting, and use a plumbline to ensure that the posts are vertical

5 Permanent angled struts can be bolted to the posts, but in the case of this decorative fence they were set in concrete then nailed to the posts

6 Use a string line stretched between the end posts to check that all the intermediate posts are properly aligned and at the correct height

7 When the concrete has set drill a 10mm hole through the top and bottom of each straining post to take the eyebolts which secure the support wires

Bernard Fallon

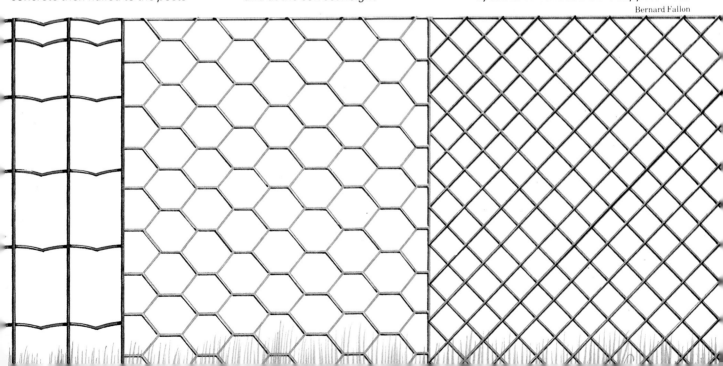

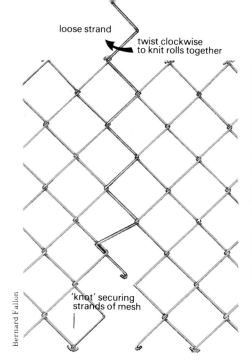

loose strand

twist clockwise to knit rolls together

'knot' securing strands of mesh

Bernard Fallon

B. *Instead of cutting chain link mesh you can break it—or knit two lengths together—by unravelling or refitting a single loosened strand*

shared boundary between yourself and your neighbours, it wise of course to seek their co-operation first. Although the deeds to your house will define the limits of your property it may still be necessary to check with the local authority surveyor's department. At the same time check the depth and direction of underground services such as water and gas pipes and drains around your property.

Having gained the approval of your neighbours and the local authority, start marking the line of the fence with string and pegs. Drive the pegs into the ground to a uniform depth so you can check easily where the ground is high or low, and use stakes 450mm high to mark the corners and changes of gradient.

If the boundary is an odd shape, or if there are frequent changes of gradient, you must decide now whether the fence would not look better and be easier to erect if the boundary followed a slightly different line.

When you have settled on the line of the fence mark the position of any gates or breaks in the perimeter. Establish the widths of the gates you intend to use and clearly mark the positions of the gate posts. Do the same at any other breaks in the fence where there are to be no gates.

You can now calculate how much wire mesh and supporting wire to buy; when ordering ask for the nearest number of full rolls so that you have a little left over. At the same time calculate how many fence posts you will need. Your first consideration must be the gate posts and the straining posts at the corners. If you are using steel or concrete fence posts,

Ray Duns

8 *If you intend using a stretcher bar to support the mesh, fix its mounting with the eyebolt and leave this loose so that you can tighten the wire*

9 *Secure the wire to the eyebolts and stretch it tight simply by tightening up the backnuts on the straining posts with a spanner*

10 *Thread the stretcher bar through the mesh at one end of the roll and bolt this to the mounting brackets on the two eyebolts*

11 *Unroll the mesh along the fence and, at the far end, unpick a knot between two strands so that you can break the mesh without cutting it*

12 *Feed a second stretcher bar through the end of the mesh and bolt this securely to the mounting brackets on the straining post*

13 *Before securing the mesh to the support wire, nail it to the intermediate fence posts using wire staples at top and bottom*

you can buy specially-designed straining posts; otherwise you may have to make up your own timber straining posts with angled bracing struts. Work out how many of these you will need and mark their positions with chalk or paint on the string lines.

Between these you must place ordinary fence posts no more than 2.8m apart, though on longer runs you may need intermediate straining posts. Mark the position of the fencing posts on the line.

The amount of support wire you need depends on the height of the fence as well as its length. Fences under 1.2m high require a wire at the top and bottom, while fences up to 2.25m high require a third support wire in the middle. Remember that you will need an eyebolt and a turnbuckle or bottlescrew for each straight line of wire to tighten it. And do not forget to order all the appropriate fittings for the straining posts and for securing the netting – these are detailed below but most suppliers will provide a complete kit with the mesh and posts.

C. *Concrete and steel fence posts are erected in the same way as timber ones, but the methods of fixing the support wires and chain link mesh are slightly different from those for timber*

Digging post holes

Aim to instal gate posts and straining posts first and dig holes both for the posts and their angled bracing struts. You can use a pick and shovel to do this, but it is easier to hire or buy a post hole digger. There are different designs available to suit most types of ground but auger or clam-shelled diggers will be perfectly adequate for most jobs.

The holes must be 600-750mm deep and about 450mm square at the top expanding to 500mm square at the bottom. For fences over 1.2m high increase the depth to about 1m. As a general rule of thumb at least one-third of the fence post should be underground.

Where the ground is rocky, remove stones and rocks by prising them out of the hole. Alternatively you can reposition the post slightly. If you cannot remove a large rock, use a star drill to make a small hole in it then mortar a steel pin in this. Drill a corresponding hole in the bottom of a timber fence post and slip it over the pin, than backfill the post hole.

Erecting fence posts

Wooden fence posts should be of pressure impregnated timber at least 100mm × 100mm in thickness, and all fence posts should be the same length. Mark the

posts with a knife cut or dab of paint at the proposed ground level so that when installed they are all the same height.

Cut angled notches in the straining and gate posts, about 300-400mm from the top, to accommodate the angled struts. Bolt the struts to the posts with coach-bolts after you have installed them.

Soak all those parts of the timber which will be below ground in creosote or a similar preservative for 24 hours before installing them (see pages 1240 to 1246). If you wish to paint them, use a preservative such as pentachlorophenol instead.

When the posts are ready slip them into their holes, packing them out with stones and gravel until they are at the correct height. Fill the hole with a relatively dry concrete mix of one part cement to six of all-in ballast and check that the posts are vertical with a plumbline or spirit level before tamping the concrete down. Leave the finished level a few millimetres above the ground to protect the posts from rot.

Keep the post level while the concrete is setting by nailing temporary braces against two adjacent faces. When all the corner posts, straining posts, and gate posts are in position and the concrete has set, instal their angled braces. Concrete them into the ground in the same way as the posts themselves, allowing two braces

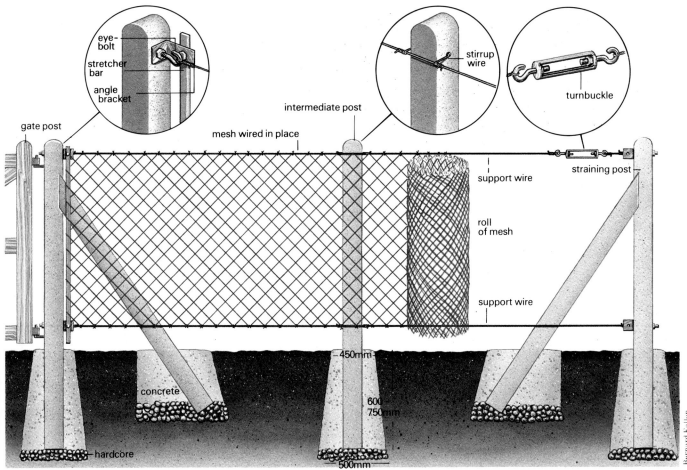

14 *Now attach the mesh to the support wires by knotting short lengths of wire around each at about 150mm intervals*

15 *To take the strain off the support wires, nail the mesh to the intermediate posts along their lengths with more wire staples*

16 *The finished fence: this one is intended only to support plants and hide a compost heap, so fence posts and braces are very light*

for corner posts and straining posts and one each for gate posts and end posts. Bolt the bracing struts to the posts first leaving the other end dangling in their holes; pack these ends out with stones and gravel, and then backfill with concrete.

Another way of fixing fence posts securely is to screw two timber battens about 600mm long to the bottom of each post before it is installed: these form a cross which cannot easily be torn out of the ground.

Fixing the mesh

You can now fit the support wire and the mesh itself. Start by drilling 10mm holes through each straining and gate post at the top and bottom, and secure two eyebolts to the post at each end of a run. Thread the end of a roll of 3mm galvanized steel wire through the eye of the upper bolt at one end of the run and twist it around itself three or four times with a pair of pliers to secure it. Run the other end of the wire to the top eyebolt at the other end of the run and either attach it to this or, if the run is a long one, attach it to a turnbuckle which has been wirelocked to the eyebolt. Tighten the wire up as much as you can and repeat this procedure at the bottom of the two end posts (fig. 9).

When the lines are tight use 15mm 16 gauge wire staples to secure them to the intervening timber fence posts. The procedure for securing the lines to metal or concrete posts is explained below.

When you fix the netting start by standing the roll upright next to the first post. Release about 600mm of the roll and align the top edge with the upper run of support wire. Staple this top corner to the post and staple the rest of the exposed end of the mesh in a vertical line down the post to the ground.

When the end is secure unroll the mesh along the line of the fence, pulling it taut as you go. Fix the mesh to the supporting wires every 150mm with a short twist of thin galvanized wire, and then staple the mesh to each post. Make sure that the mesh pattern remains regular and is not distorted by too much tension.

Do not bend the mesh around corners. Instead cut the roll by unravelling two spirals of the mesh and staple the loose end to the post concerned. Because of the structure of chainlink mesh unravelling it is very easy: use a pair of pliers to loosen the 'knots' at top and bottom of one strand of wire and untwist the wire from the mesh by turning it anti-clockwise. You can repair a fence or join two rolls together by reversing this procedure.

Steel and concrete posts: Although you can staple mesh to timber fence posts you cannot do this with steel and concrete units. Nor can you easily drill them to accommodate eyebolts and supporting struts. The majority of steel and concrete posts are pre-drilled for this purpose. But securing the mesh remains a problem.

Instal the fence posts as described above, aligning the pre-drilled holes along the line of the run. Insert the eyebolts in the end posts as normal, but use them to secure an angled steel bracket to the posts at the same level as the support wires. Instal and secure the support wires as normal, but fix them to the intermediate posts by running a stirrup wire through the holes in the post to hold the support wire on each side of them (fig. C).

Unroll the first 600mm of mesh and align the top edge with the top support wire. Thread a length of 20mm × 5mm steel bar the same height as the straining post through the mesh at this end and bolt it to the angled brackets.

Run the mesh to the other straining post on the run and secure it there with a similar steel bar. Secure the mesh to the support wires in the normal manner, and wirelock the mesh to the posts.

Some fencing kits with steel fence posts are supplied with different fixtures to replace the eyebolts and turnbuckles, but instructions should be supplied with the equipment, and in any case the principles of erecting a fence are identical whichever equipment you use.

Special considerations

Where you are building a pen for animals such as dogs and rabbits which may burrow their way out under the fence it is a good idea to purchase fence posts and mesh that are about 300mm higher than you require. Dig a trench 250mm deep and 100mm wide along the line of the proposed fence and dig the post holes in the bottom of this. Erect the fence as normal, but turn the mesh in slightly at the bottom of the trench and replace the soil you have dug up.

You can prevent the onset of damp and rot in timber fence posts by capping them as described on pages 1240 to 1247, but it will occasionally become necessary to replace one. In this case loosen the eyebolts at the end of the affected run and remove the staples securing the support wires and mesh to the damaged post. Dig out the post and fit a new one at the same height as the others, staple the wires and mesh back in place, and tighten up the support wires again.

If the netting sags due to vandalism or people attempting to climb over the fence you must rehang it. Remove all the tie wires holding the mesh to the support wires and also the staples securing it to the intermediate posts. Afterwards, working from one end to the other, pull the mesh tight and refix it.